ANITA
GARIBALDI

Anthony Valerio's biography of Anita Garibaldi is exactly what she would have wanted--a story told with sensitivity and eloquence and one that positions her as the active agent of her own destiny.

--Professor Philip V. Cannistraro

BY THE SAME AUTHOR

The Mediterranean Runs Through Brooklyn

Valentino and the Great Italians

Conversation with Johnny

BART: A Life of A. Bartlett Giamatti

Anita Garibaldi, a Biography

The Little Sailor, a Romantic Thriller

Toni Cade Bambara's One Sicilian Night

John Dante's Inferno, a Playboy's Life

Dante in Love

IMMIGRANTS, according to Anthony Valerio (vols. 1 & 2)

ANITA GARIBALDI, a Biography Copyright© 2013, 2019, 2020 Daisy H Productions, LLC and Anthony Valerio. All rights reserved. No portion reof this book may be reproduced, by any process or technique, without the express written consent of the author.

Publishing History: Praeger, 2000; Gallucci editore, 2017.
Cover: Sculpture of Anita Garibaldi by Antônio caringi (1905-1981), Rio Grande do Sul.
Cover photo of statue, Ruy Luiz Machado
Cover design©Dave Barry©20/20
ISBN: 978-0-9904675-0-2

In gratitude to Dr. Anthony Campanella & the Garibaldi family & by no means lastly, for my great friend & scholar Philip V. Cannistraro

Critics are saying—

"In Valerio's hand, Anita Garibaldi emerges as the courageous but vulnerable woman from Brazil, whose singular and precious spirit was caught in the times. Anita Garibaldi is a romance discovered in history's embrace. Valerio creates the Brazilian ethos in its emerald presence as the brilliant nerve in Garibaldi's brave but short time. This biography has a texture like a Renoir film, broad and expansive, swimming along in voluble seas."—Afaa M. Weaver, (formerly) Simmons College, Boston

"Anthony Valerio's genre-crossing biography provides unique insight into Anita Garibaldi's 'short, glorious life.' Valerio writes with a novelist's dedication to character and an historian's dedication to the past. An unusual book for a revolutionary woman."-Janet R. Jacobson, Director Center for Research on Women. Barnard College

It's thanks to Anthony Valerio that Anita has restored to her her personality and her life, bound to, but not confused with, the myth of Garibaldi --Emilio Gentile

TABLE OF CONTENTS

Preface

PART 1: Brazil (1821-41)

PART II: Uruguay (1841-48)

PART III: Italy (1848-49)

PART IV: The Retreat (July-August 1849)

Epilogue

Chronology of the Life of Anita Garibaldi

Further Reading

Acknowledgements

She's an amalgam of two elemental forces: the strength and courage of a man, the character and tenderness of a woman, symbolized by the daring and vigor with which she brandished her sword and the beautiful oval of her face that trimmed the softness of her extraordinary eyes.--Luigi Rossetti

She had become, from the habits of her country, a splendid horsewoman, and it was a sight to be remembered as she rode a curveting animal by the side of her husband.--Rear-Admiral H.F Winnington Ingram

I don't see her any longer as a victim. Nor can I see her as a heroine. In this she was totally different from him [G. Garibaldi]. She wasn't fighting for theirs and their children's future. Had that been the case it would have made more common sense for him not to acquiesce to her final demand to follow him, which cost her her life. But at that point her identity was so totally merged with his that to deny her her wish would have been to kill her even more brutally. By keeping her with him he honored her sacrifice and cleared his own conscience all at the same time. I guess her death could be called a martyrdom of love.--Maria Inês Lacey

PREFACE

Today her body rests atop the Janiculum Hill, at the foot of the huge bronze equestrian monument to her memory designed by sculptor Mario Rutelli.

For almost a decade after her death in 1849, her remains lay in a grave in the village of Mandriole, on the eastern coast of Italy, where her desperate husband had been forced to bury her during his frantic escape following the collapse of the Roman Republic. In 1859, Garibaldi had her body disinterred and moved to his own birthplace, the city of Nice. It remained there for the next eighty years, buried in what became foreign territory after Nice became a French possession in 1860.

Anita Garibaldi was brought back to her husband's homeland--not to her own, which was on another continent in a different hemisphere--for the dedication of the Rutelli monument. The ceremonies took place on June 4, 1932, almost fifty years to the day of Giuseppe Garibaldi's death, and shortly before the opening of festivities to celebrate the tenth anniversary of the Fascist seizure of power. Present, along with the large crowd that had gathered for the occasion, were three special figures: Victor Emmanuel III, grandson of the man who became king of Italy as a result of Garibaldi's exploits in

1860; General Ezio Garibaldi, grandson of Anita and Giuseppe; and Benito Mussolini, the *Duce* of Fascism and the real ruler of Italy.

Earlier that same day, Fascist police agents had stopped and arrested a suspicious young man named Angelo Sbartellotto in Piazza Venezia. He was found carrying a pistol and a bomb. Under intense interrogation, and most probably after having been tortured, Sbartellotto confessed to being an anarchist and that he had returned secretly to Italy from France in order to assassinate Mussolini while the dictator was delivering his remarks about Anita during the ceremonies on the Janiculum. The Fascists executed Sbartellotto a few weeks later.

The speech that Mussolini gave before Anita's monument was very much a Fascist speech, and it revealed the difficult dilemma that even in death Anita Garibaldi posed for Italian authorities.[1] For Mussolini, Anita was an uncomfortable legacy. Her husband had, of course, been a great national hero--perhaps *the* greatest figure of the nation's modern history, and Anita herself had died while fighting alongside him during a critical moment in the country's *Risorgimento*, its struggle for freedom against foreign rule. Fascism had embraced Giuseppe Garibaldi as an Italian hero in the tradition of Caesar--and, presumably, of Mussolini himself. Several of his and Anita's grandsons had fought in World War I and had been prominently associated with the Fascist cause. For a regime that prided itself on acting the protector of its nationals living abroad, the reclaiming of Anita's body from foreign soil had been an act of historical vindication.

But now, in 1932, in the midst of the long dark Fascist

nightmare that had descended on Italy, Mussolini was supposed to honor Anita in a very public ceremony, one in which both he and the king were no doubt reluctant participants. Simply put, the problem was that Anita Garibaldi had represented everything that Fascism detested: she had been a most unconventional woman who had violated the very core of gender principles that the misogynist Fascist regime was trying to impose on Italian women--she had been a female warrior, but Fascism insisted that men were soldiers and women mothers; technically she had been a bigamist and the mother of illegitimate children, while Fascism privileged religion, conventional sexual mores, and family values; she was born a foreigner, most probably of mixed racial heritage, while Fascism was blindly chauvinistic and racist; she had believed in and acted on a set of radical revolutionary ideals, while Fascism had come to power as a right-wing reaction against radicalism, and Anita had been a true internationalist, while Fascism proclaimed the doctrine of national primacy.

Mussolini solved his dilemma in part by giving the commission for the statue to a sculptor whose training belonged to the 19th-century academic tradition, and whose earlier work had been devoted to designing nationalist monuments. In truth the image of Anita that Rutelli fashioned reflected the ironies of her life--a gaucho warrior and her galloping horse, but with her arms wrapped protectively around her children. And the *Duce's* speech was a tour de force of dissimulation: the three sentences actually devoted to Anita in his 20-minute speech underscored how she "always reconciled during her swift and adventurous life her high duties as a mother with those of an intrepid fighter at the side of Garibaldi." The remainder of Mussolini's talk focused on Garibaldi himself and the way in which the Red Shirts had been precursors of the Fascist Black Shirts.[2]

Anita Garibaldi had been born Ana Maria de Jésus in Brazil, and she met Garibaldi in 1839 when she was about eighteen. For both of them it had seemed entirely natural that they--one Italian, the other Brazilian--would fight on behalf of a local independence movement. The first half of the 19th century was an age of revolutionary internationalism, when the ideals of romanticism and democratic sovereignty were inspiring nationalist uprisings throughout Europe and Latin America.

Garibaldi himself had been a follower of the revolutionary Giuseppe Mazzini. Born in 1807 in Nice, then a possession of the king of Piedmont-Sardinia, Garibaldi spent his youth as a merchant seaman sailing the Mediterranean. It was not until he was in his twenties, however, that he developed a political consciousness. The *Risorgimento* had its immediate roots during the upheavals of the French Revolution and Napoleon's campaigns in Italy in the 1790s. After the defeat of Napoleon, the great powers had met at the Congress of Vienna in 1814-16 to restore the rulers of Italy and other regions of Europe to their legitimate thrones and to stamp out any remnants of revolutionary spirit, The earliest stirrings of resistance against the restoration in the Italian states came in 1820-21, when revolutions broke out in Naples and Piedmont, but these were crushed by Austrian armies. Further abortive insurrections were put down in 1830a-31, and it was then that Mazzini founded his revolutionary organization Young Italy and gave Italian radicals a coherent ideology based on the principles of popular insurrection, political democracy, and republican ideals.

Between 1831-33, Garibaldi began to gravitate to the patriot movement. He was particularly struck by the brutal repression of a failed Mazzini revolt in Piedmont in 1833, and that same year, he encountered the Utopian Socialist ideas of Saint Simon. That summer, when his ship docked at Marseilles, Garibaldi was introduced to Mazzini, who was in exile there after having been condemned to death in absentia by King Charles Albert of Piedmont-Sardinia. It was then, in January-February 1834, that Garibaldi became a member of Young Italy and agreed to take part in still another revolutionary plot hatched by Mazzini: while a revolutionary force would strike at Savoy from Switzerland, Garibaldi would foment a mutiny among sailors of the Sardinian navy in Genoa. Like the others, this insurrection also fizzled. Although Garibaldi managed to escape, he, too, was condemned to death in absentia. In the late summer of 1834, Garibaldi decided to go to South America where a large Italian population, including political refugees, had already migrated. He shipped out of Marseilles under the name Giuseppe Pane and in November arrived at the port of Rio de Janeiro.

Garibaldi remained in South America for the next fourteen years. In Rio de Janeiro he made contact with other Italian refugees and joined the local branch of Young Italy. For a time he earned a living as a tradesman for Italian food products, but he bristled in inactivity and in May 1837 he entered the service of the republic of Rio Grande do Sul in its struggle to gain independence from Brazil. As a privateer armed with letters of marque from the rebel government, he outfitted a ship, dubbed the *Mazzini,* and fought a number of naval engagements along the coast. In need of provisions, Garibaldi entered Uruguayan waters and anchored in the port of Maldonado, at the entrance of the River Plate, but when local officials sympathetic to Brazil sought to arrest him he traveled up river past Montevideo and was seriously wounded in battle. In June, he made his way to the town of Gualeguay, Argentina, where he was captured and remained for six months on his word not to try to escape. In December or early January, however, he attempted to elude his guards and was recaptured. After suffering torture at the hands of a brutal commandant, Garibaldi was imprisoned for some months, only to be unexpectedly released.

It was not long before Garibaldi rejoined the fighting, this time going overland into Rio Grande do Sul and looking up Bento Gonçalves, president of the breakaway republic. Gonçalves secured two ships, one for Garibaldi, who now received a commission as commander of naval forces for the republic, and one for an idealistic young North American named John Griggs. The two officers raided Brazilian merchant ships along the coast, and were to participate in an ambitious plan to wrest control of the state of Santa Catarina, north of

Rio Grande, from Brazil. In July 1839, after a spectacular operation in which Garibaldi had their two ships hauled overland from a lagoon to the Atlantic, his vessel foundered in a violent storm and he lost half his crew. With the remaining ship, however, he and Griggs led a sea assault on the port of Laguna while Gonçalves attacked from land. Garibaldi was among the victorious rebel forces that entered the town on July 22, 1839.

Over the next several months Garibaldi conducted raids on Brazilian shipping from his base in Laguna. It was on his return from one of these forays that Garibaldi and Anita met. And it is here that Anthony Valerio's story of Anita begins.

Even if she had lived into old age, as Garibaldi did, it is a story that Anita herself could not have told. Anita was illiterate, and while she eventually learned to sign her name haltingly to the bottom of a few letters that she dictated to others, documents record little direct sounds of her own voice. Garibaldi himself, in his autobiography written many years later, composed a moving portrait of Anita, and his biographers have included accounts of his relationship with Anita in their books. But Anthony Valerio has given Anita a voice of her own for the first time. Although there have been studies about her published in Portuguese and a joint portrait of Garibaldi and Anita in Italian, this is the first book to privilege Anita as the center of a story of which Garibaldi was a part but not the focus.

Anita's story could not, of course, be told without reference to Garibaldi. It is unlikely, in fact, that Anita would have expected or wanted the story of her life separated from his. Theirs was a passionate love affair, as well as a partnership, and the relationship was shockingly unconventional, especially for the times. The romance was "romantic" in the way in which Romantic writers of the age liked to structure such stories--she the beautiful young woman of the tropics, never entirely comfortable in society, he a dashing seaman and soldier of growing reputation who moved easily among guerilla fighters in the jungles as well as in the more sophisticated world of the rich and famous. Despite these differences, for much of their time together they treated each other as equals, as comrades sharing the dangers of war and faith in a set of common political values.

Yet the partnership between Anita and Garibaldi was not entirely equal. One gets the impression that for Garibaldi his life with Anita was a particular moment--in truth an important and emotionally powerful moment--in his life. In later years he went on to have children with three other women, two of whom he married. For Anita, on the other hand, Garibaldi seems to have become the essential focus of her life, and his attractiveness to other women at times caused her to experience fits of jealousy.

The partnership also unbalanced itself in a more serious way. As his fame grew, he increasingly overshadows her, and Anthony Valerio himself alerts us to the fact that as it moves forward there is less and less about her in the story. And when slowly we come to realize the reason for Anita's disappearance from the center of events, our admiration for the "modern" nature of the relationship they fashioned begins to founder--between 1840 and 1847, Anita gave birth to four children conceived with Garibaldi, and this essential fact seems to have inexorable altered the balance in their relationship. When they settled in Montevideo, most of Anita's time and energy was consumed with raising their children and maintaining the household, and when they decided to leave for Italy in 1848 it had been determined that she and the children would stay with his mother in Nice while he went to war. Anita did eventually leave the children with her mother-in-law and join Garibaldi in Rome, but the decision was hers, and he was not happy about it. It was, at the end, a decision that led to her death.

It is perhaps the final irony of Anita's life that the monument that Mussolini erected to her memory almost a century later captured not only the values of his own anti-feminist regime, but the tensions that shadowed the life of a woman caught in the gender-bound world of her age. From this perspective, one suspects that Anthony Valerio's biography of Anita Garibaldi is exactly what she would have wanted--a story told with sensitivity and eloquence and one that positions her as the active agent of her own destiny.

--Philip V. Cannistraro, former Distinguished Professor of History, Queens College, City University of New York

Notes to Preface

1. In 1929, while it was still in the planning stage, Mussolini had had to defend the monument to Anita in the wake of remarks of Pope Pius XI that the Lateran Accords between Italy and the Vatican had made the statue "inopportune." See Mussolini's speech, "Relazione all Camera dei Deputati sugli accordi del Laterano," May 13, 1929, in *Opera Omnia di Benito Mussolini*, XXIV (Florence, 1958), 89.

2. "Epopea Garibaldina," June 4, 1932, *Opera Omnia di Benito Mussolini*, XXV (Florence, 1958), 108-11.

PART 1: BRAZIL (1821-1841)

1. A CHILDHOOD

Her mother, Maria Antônia de Jesus, is a neglected character in the saga of her life, as if the mother wouldn't have as much to do with her relationship with Garibaldi as the father. Stately, beautiful, Maria Bento came from the civilized world of the city, São Paulo, and could speak correct Portuguese, affecting a way her healthy, good-looking daughters were able to speak. Why Maria Bento moved from the city to the country isn't known. Often, city folks moved to the country because of business reverses, and in the country the cultivated young women met the half-savage, strong men of the *pampas* and fell in love and married, and this love and the beauty of nature all around replaced even distant memories of the city. In the mountains of southern Brazil, province of Santa Catarina, Maria Bento had two daughters, Manuela and Felicidade, followed by a son who didn't survive his first winter. It's said that Maria Bento wanted another son. When she announced she was pregnant, the family moved down to the valley. Their wagon and two-wheel oxcart rambled down steep slopes, across deep gullies and swollen rivers. From the ridge, the family could see the Atlantic. They settled in Morrinhos, a trading settlement, and Bentão Ribeiro da Silva built a cabin on wooden piles in a clearing of banana trees, on the left bank of the Tubarão, or Shark, River.

Ana Maria de Jesus Ribeiro da Silva, called Aninha, was born a few minutes before midnight on August 21, 1821. August was a bad-luck month. What bad things were going to happen? the villagers whispered.

In her little, shared room, home arrived with the aroma of coffee, the cock crowing and *Ben-ti-vis* singing in the distance, "I-caught-you, I-caught-you..." When she was a baby, her father took her for rides on his favorite gelding, *Piña*. Her long, black hair fell all around her face and she laughed and slept in Bentão's left arm set across the saddlebow. He nuzzled his great bearded face against the soft skin of her cheek, asked for a kiss. She kissed his wooly cheek. With the settling in of the black night, color of her hair, Bentão took her outside and pointed up. She looked up at the Southern Cross, Three Marias, forever dying Diamond of Venus. They went outside the next night and the next--she looked up and saw how the constellations had moved.

Bentão was a *tropeiro*, herder of cattle, sheep and horses. He was one of a band of neighboring herdsmen, like the men of most Brazilian villages rode out on hunts for meat, hides and tallow, plumes of the America rhea sought after by European ladies and wild horses to be used in future drives. Each drover and cavalryman rode *cavalhadas*, with two spare horses. Her father needed his horses. He'd taught her to whistle--now she whistled and their horses appeared from around the bend in the river, out from among the banana trees. The horses strained into formation, geldings of the same color following the white bell mare who could be seen at night. The horses galloped up, stood still. Bentão pointed to his first mount and she saddled her carefully, for when the 40-pound saddle was spread out, it had to make a comfortable bed for her father. First she spread on sweatcloths, then several *matras* of colored wool and a corona of leather. A pair of padded leather cylinders held parallel by straps fit along each side of the withers and backbone. Then she lay on a leather square to which she attached the stirrup leathers and a wide cinch. Tightening the cinch kept the saddle from turning. She spread on a sheepskin, wool side up. A leather cover with girth secured the last two layers. Finally, she attached the *laço* to the cinch ring.

She packed her father's other weapons--*facão*, or long knife, bamboo spear twin-tipped with crescents of sharpened steel and his *bolas*, the drover's and cavalryman's main weapon. The *bolas* was called with affection *"Tres Marias,"* after the constellation, because of its three, six-foot strips of plaited rawhide. These were joined together at one end like a chainshot, and attached to each free end was a round weight of stone or lead or bone shrunk into a rawhide pocket. Holding a smaller ball in hand, the horseman whirled the other balls around his head, raising a speeding, whirring, deadly symphony--and then hurled his *bolas* 50 to 75 yards with uncanny accuracy, entangling the legs of the flying calf or rhea or enemy horse, and the prey went down, rolling, fluttering, panting.

She worked with her father cutting away trees and bush for pasture, with the herds, the corral built of pine. She gentled the wild colts her father brought home. No one except the young, agile, black professional horsebreakers rivaled her in gentling a colt. She sprung onto his back which had never known bit or spur or saddle. She rushed madly with him, holding onto his mane, her legs clasped around him with the grip of a vise, striking, spurring. She leapt into the air with him, rolled over with him and then rose with the colt streaming with sweat now, breathless, white with foam, legs trembling. Overpowered, the colt flew off like an arrow, in a few minutes covered a great expanse of land, then returned with the same swiftness. In three days she bitted, saddled and mounted the colt on the open plain.

She was ten years old.

Her father spoke of their ancestors, islanders of the Azores. They were a plain, tough, adaptable, honorable people, and vigilant, having kept a watchful eye on fiery craters and cinder cones, at times a pleased eye on the surface calm of crater lakes reflecting passing clouds, rays of the sun and moon and shooting stars. Like the stronger horses captured by the marauding imperial guerrilla Pedro de Abreu, called "Moringue, the marten" for his craftiness, who before galloping off killed the weaker horses, choice Azorean couples had been paid to migrate. They came to Brazil South in whaling ships, charged with spreading the conquest and defending the frontier. These rustics-soldiers settled the coastal town Laguna--it was the frontier then--and then crossed 600 leagues of frightening desert and explored and settled the high plateaus and vast, virgin plains, the green *pampas,* Guicha word for "space". With 200 Paulistas of the citizen-soldier Cristovão Pareira, and 254 men from captaincies under Silva Pais, about 500 Azorean couples drifted south and founded the settlement-fort at the mouth of the *Logoa dos Patos,* Lagoon of the Ducks. Her ancestors had doubled as soldiers, in an instant putting down hoe and *laço* and picking up lance and musket, then, bundling in leather, they rode out and defended against the Castilians from Buenos Aires, Guaranís of the Reductions and remnants of the scattered, decimated Indian tribes on the hunt for wild cattle.

The Spanish and Portuguese conquerors had come without women. They coupled with women of the Guaraní, Tepé and Minuano nations, and with African women brought on ships twice a year, untaxed, to the Spanish Jesuits. "Sturdy women so clean of body," King Manuel I's scribe wrote back to him, "lusty females wearing the very shadow of the forest in the color of their skin." Then came the Islander women, already married, and finally single women called *mazuelas,* invited by the brigadier to come seek married status.

The family was poor. Maria Bento hired herself out as a domestic. Felicidade and Manuela went to one in a system of public schools initiated by the crown in 1826. Aninha stayed home and cared for her brothers who had been born in quick succession, strengthening the bond with her father. But Salvador and Bernardo had to be given away, to a Captain Aborim and his wife.

King Dom João of Brazil, who ruled over two million slaves, had envisioned his slaves fleeing across the southern border to Uruguay. Uruguay had abolished slavery and had decreed that any slave who set foot on Uruguay's soil was free. Drawing on the

Southerners' heritage of vigilance, violence and war, João invaded the young republic of Uruguay, initiating 11 years of continual warfare (1817-28). Eighty-five percent of his troops came from the South. As a result of the war, the South's population was decimated, its public treasury exhausted, its cities destroyed--cities the seeds of which had been the corrals their ancestors had put up along the cattle, mule and horse drives to the Sorocoba meat markets up north around the gold, silver and diamond mines. High taxes were levied on hides, leather and *charque*, or meat. Their land was covered with the carcasses of wild cattle, often killed for one steak and left for the carrion crows.

Within a year, Salvador and Bernardo died of pernicious fever. They'd been given away out of poverty and returned home in small pine boxes. She blamed god and the crown, for the rest of her life wondered how her brothers might have turned out.

It hadn't been a year since her brothers and Bentão's sons died, when one day after working with the herds Bentão rode to the new *galpão*, large storehouse, going up. *Galpãos* were used for jerking and drying beef, in time of war for storing *yerba maté*, charcoal and weapons, iron and steel. Bentão climbed onto the roof. A beam split underfoot and he went crashing down straight into a jagged beam, which pierced his heart.

Scene straight out of a western movie long before they were made: man of the house late, women waiting, fixing the dress for the village dance, making cheese. Hushed voices outside filter in-- neighboring herdsmen. The women rush to the door, span it, watch in horror as the body covered except for the head is taken off the mule-drawn cart on a rough litter, then into the house, passing the women, and into the kitchen. Tragedy must unfold in the woman's place. The men tell the story gently, with pain, as if wooden stakes had been driven through *their* hearts.

What does a 12-year-old who feels loved by and loves her father feel that day and all the days, months, years that follow?

Losing her father amounted to losing her reasons to exist. Those things she considered lost would never be found again. In the company of her father she'd been able to talk, even be outspoken, and no one disrespected her. She lost the thrill of being truthful--there'd been no reason to lie. Now she was just a 12-year-old girl no one listened to.

It took some time for her heart's fissure to deepen and break. A new *tropeiro* took her father's place and she continued to work with him, and continued to fish with her sisters and cook, do chores, with her mother. From her broken heart issued a vast silence. This silence took on dimensions of place, a great barren plain seen only by her inner eye, lit only by the light of this eye. Words as men knew them weren't spoken there. Words were replaced by her own inner strength.

It was the custom that three months after a death, on the Sunday closest to it, a Requiem Mass was said and afterwards friends visited, bringing food. Bentão may have wished she stay in the house-- but she walked downstream to her favorite spot, her rock close to the water. She cried, idly tossing white stones, and cooled her face.

Suddenly, an unwelcome hand on her shoulder--Pedro's, a neighboring farmhand.

She longed for tenderness but not from Pedro. He was still the way he was before her father died--vulgar, smelly, face and arms piled with hair. She tried to walk away but Pedro grabbed her and forced her down, edged her toward a tree, pinned her arms and crushed her chest. She relaxed her body. Pedro relaxed. She twisted out from under and ran.

The next Sunday she took out Piña. A thick rope barred the way between the settlement and the church, one end looped around a tree trunk, the other end hitched to a team of oxen huddled on the roadside. Pedro sat against a tree, back to her. She pulled in the reins, whirled, drove straight for the oxen. Pedro tried to head off her charge, grabbing the bit. She whipped him across the jaw, then rode off.

Pedro went to the Justice of the Peace, displayed his gash. She was brought in and questioned in front of her mother. She said nothing. The Justice respected the dignity of her silence and interpreted her violent act as one of revenge for the previous assault, which he and the village elders had heard about. Perhaps no one listened to her now but the Justice had listened to Bentão, and their friendship extended to his widow and daughters. She was let off.

Felicidade married a ship caulker from Rio de Janeiro, and Manuela went off to train with a famous midwife who'd come from France. Maria Bento sold the horses, paid off debts and, with her youngest, migrated south to the sea level, the farming settlement of Carniça, where they received support and comfort from godfather João Braga and his family. Then they traveled two more miles to the seaport, Laguna, where the first Azorean couples had come. Powerless and penniless, mother and daughter settled into two rooms on *Rua Rincoã,* close to the harbor.

2. A GIRL WITHOUT A FATHER

It's been imagined that she was able to read and write, perhaps to be more like us. At first, in Laguna, she dictated letters to her good friend Maria da Gloria Garcia, the postmaster's daughter, then in Montevideo began teaching herself to read and write. She began to write about a year before her death, in Italy, signing one letter to Garibaldi, "Anita Garibau."

Her first letter in Laguna was from sister Felicidade, she recognized the name. Holding the letter tight, she ran to her friend Maria da Gloria's house. Maria read the letter, then took her dictation:

"Just imagine how wonderful it would be to do as you please!

"For example, help *Tio Antonio* [their uncle] prepare for the revolution. *Tio* told me after the revolution we'll be able to pay a doctor to take care of mother. She's always tired, it's obvious she works too hard... People never seem to think I'm okay. I walk around alone with my eyes up, make faces, my skirt's too short, I wiggle my hips--the tongues are always wagging..."

Tio Antonio had a mule franchise in the mountain district and belonged to the exalted liberal party made up of people from all classes, civilians and soldiers, men of the city and men of the country. The crown called them "*farrapos,*" meaning "people in rags". *Tio* was impatient with the *farrapos'* efforts of negotiating with the crown over land rights, choices of provincial presidents and local franchises, especially the mule franchise. Mountain trails were scaled with mules, communication between villages facilitated by mules. But after the Uruguayan war, the mule franchise was taken away. *Tio* hadn't seen his niece since her father died, didn't see her now walking alone with her eyes up, making faces and wiggling her hips with her skirt too short.

There were more men than women in Laguna but this happy circumstance for eligible young women was dimmed by their mothers, who felt fishermen and port workers were too poor, and soldiers of the National Guard had one thing on their minds and it wasn't marriage. Becoming a wife, caretaker for life, was the natural thing to do, especially for a girl approaching her fourteenth birthday who didn't have a father--a girl without a father was like a gaucho without his horse, nothing--a girl who recently had to horse-whip a man to keep him off, a girl whose natural outspoken nature had blossomed again, and her body ripened.

She was 5 feet 3 inches tall; dark complexion; oval-shape face; large, dark, slanting eyes; black hair often in braids down to her waist; large bosom.

Women drew water from two fountains on the *morro da barra*-- the high, rocky, curving hill protecting Laguna from the sea winds. The main fountain was near the foot of the hill, close to the beach. Moving up the curving, jagged path bordered by flaming bougainvillea swaying in the sea breezes was a smaller fountain in a clearing of trees, near the summit. The women needed time to fill their pitchers and pails, and strong arms to carry them.

Shoemaker Manuel Duarte de Aguiar saw her at the main fountain, every day after that waited for her. One mid-day he approached her and asked to carry her filled pitcher and pail.

She said nothing, just looked at him. Duarte seemed meek, sad, closed up like a mollusk, terribly thin, black oily hair. It gave her the shivers just to look at him. She turned and walked away, carrying her own pail, balancing her own pitcher.

Manuel Duarte sought the higher authority of the mother. He courted the tired, overworked Maria Bento, presenting himself as owner of his own house on the *barra*, close to the beach; and owner of his own shop behind the main market, just like the wealthy furniture- and clock-makers vacationing in Laguna who had shops in the big cities. He himself came from a big city, the capital, Destêrro, and he had a carpenter friend who could repair their furniture come down damaged from Morrinhos. He could make them new shoes. His reputation for drink was true but he promised to stop drinking at the altar because their children would not be known for their love of drink.

Maria Bento promised her youngest to Manuel Duarte.

She continued to fetch water but now from the small fountain near the summit. The noon sun was ablaze when sergeant of the National Guard, Gonçalves Padilha, asked to carry her pail and pitcher. She looked at Padilha hard, then walked into the flowering trees and disappeared.

The gallant sergeant appealed to godfather João Braga, who said she'd been promised to another.

On August 21, 1835, her fourteenth birthday, Father Dom Manuel Francisco Cruz married Manuel Duarte and Ana Maria de Jésus Ribeiro da Silva in *Sant'Antonio dos Anjos*. One of the white satin slippers Duarte had made her came off at the church door. An old woman approached, shaking her head, intoning: "Bad omen, poor girl..."

A reception was held in the large mud hut across from the church. Duarte drank. On his wedding night, he fell asleep drunk. She was closed up like a mollusk anyway. It took Duarte two weeks to pry open his bride.

3. THE GIFT OF LAND

"The *farrapos* took Porto Alegre..."

She waited...

Her tears fell into her plate, on the dirty clothes she washed. But she held on to her inner wisdom and common sense, and in her heart and imagination was still free. She gave Duarte ultimatums about his drinking and, while he faced losing his *cometa* for life on the wagon, she lived with her mother and godfather Braga. She kept up her friendships.

By day her good friend Maria da Gloria helped her father sort the mail and by night, in the light of candles, opened letters and read bulletins. Maria shared the news with her young friend, who also spoke to sailors making regular runs along the coast.

Underground newspaper *O Continentino* reported collective revolts in the northern provinces of Maranhão and Para, pacified by army marshal José de Souza Soares Andréia--"pacified," that is, wiped out, particularly the Black Guard of Para along the Amazon who'd fought with clubs and razors and the ancient, African, lightning-fast method of combat *capoeira,* using the feet that held knives. The revolution moved south. The crown contemptuously flouted the *farrapos'* one-year effort at negotiating and on September 20, one month after her marriage, their neighbors to the north, the *farrapos* of Rio Grande, broke from the empire. *Tio Antonio* planned to join the siege of Porto Alegre, Rio Grande's capital. In the light of a candle she dictated to Maria da Gloria:

Do you think I can go? I've had a lot of time to think and now I'm sure you've always been right--one shouldn't tolerate a government that's distant, unjust, exploitive. I want to be part of the rebellion so that I can have a sense of doing something useful. I wouldn't be a simple *ospedera* [cook, wash clothes], I could be one of the men.

She didn't join the siege. She was afraid, a 14-year-old girl alone with gaucho guerrillas in the mountains.

She waited...

The *farrapos* took Porto Alegre, declared independence and elected Bento Gonçalves da Silva president.

But then the *farrapos* were defeated at the Battle of Fanfa, near Fanfa Island. President Gonçalves was captured and imprisoned in Fort Laje, an island near the entrance to Rio de Janeiro. *Tio Antonio's* house was burned down.

"I want to kill the men who burned down your house."

She waited...

Moderate and monarchic liberals changed sides but the revolution continued. It had a base, the small highland village of Piratini. The new Republic of Rio Grande was supported by practically all its 160,000 citizens, 20% joined the army. An army of four brigades included 14-year-old boys. In addition to a president, the Republic had four vice-presidents, first three and then six ministers, chamber of deputies and a senate. While Bento Gonçalves was in prison, acting president Gomes Jardin decreed a pension for widows and orphans on the order of one half the fallen soldier's wage. The Republic had its own post office and *paradeiros*, horse-changing posts for document transfers and its own flag, hymn, coat-of-arms. Through their suffering and bloodshed, her and the other Southerners' ancestors had earned for them the title of "citizen".

People of the South lived by legends. Legends were their bible. The legend told throughout the land now was Bento Gonçalves' escape from Fort Lajes prison.

In the 1770's, Bento's father had conquered the land between Jalvi and Commaquà controlled by the Spanish Missions, and awarded *sesmarias*, huge land tracts, to relatives and friends, all Brazilians. Like his father and hers, Bento began as a *tropeiro*, herder, then married the daughter of the great cattle smuggler Nariso Garcia, a Spaniard. Bento had served in the imperial army against Uruguay and commanded the imperial National Guard. How to get rid of such an important man? Sweet cakes shot with arsenic and doused with onion, the Count de Lages, minister of war, decided.

Bento sniffed the sweetcakes but didn't like what he smelled, so he tossed them to the dog with him--prison regulations a bit more lax than we know them today. The poor dog ate the cakes, rolled his eyes, went stiff.

Bento hid the dog. When the guard came to collect the plates, he found the prisoner doubled over, clutching his stomach--urgent business. Bento was taken down to the beach. He dragged his legs on the sand, collapsing now and then on his way to the water. He dove in, currents drew him out--to his death, the guard figured.

Bento swam and found a boat, then horses. He rode *cavalhados*, with spare horses, from Rio de Janeiro to the South, cutting a swath through the land that was gift to all.

Bento Gonçalves's escape was an inspiration. Rio Grande's Republican government had packed its archives in wagons and followed the army into the mountains--the same course, she and Maria da Glória noted, followed by the Republican government of the United States when its capital, Philadelphia, was threatened by the British army. Now 2,000 gauchos, finest horsemen in the world and monarchs of the knife, waited in the mountains to take up arms again.

4. REVOLUTION IN EXCHANGE

"Rumor had it that Garibaldi had transported his lanchas, gunboats, over land to Lake Tramandai."

A wife without children was like a gaucho without his horse, nothing, so when four years of marriage didn't produce a child, she was disgraced. Maria Bento moved back to Carniça with godfather Braga; and in Year IV of the Revolution, May 1839, Manuel Duarte rode off alone with the cavalry of the national guard.

The imperial government sent 6,000 well-equipped troops against the *farrapos* and they had 1,827 cavalry and 2,247 infantry, which included the marines. The armies traveled great distances in search of and in retreat from the enemy. For the rebels, the custom was for women and, if they had them, children, to go to war with their men. Women "walked" like the food, herds of cattle and oxen. The shoemaker Manuel Duarte didn't ask his wife to go with him.

Rather than live among painful memories in Duarte's house, she chose to live with friends Henrique and Miguela, shopkeepers, in their low, simple house surrounded by orange and mango groves, near the top of the hill. In exchange for cooking, fetching water and washing clothes, she was allowed to ride Henrique's horse. Often she rode to the cemetery in Morinhos to visit with her father.

The rebels in place in Laguna held nocturnal meetings in the postmaster's office, Maria da Gloria presiding, her dark hand lighting candles with a long wooden match. Maria's fiancé was present. The names of other rebels in place aren't known. It turned out they weren't needed for the first surprise assault, so they remain patriots without names. The nameless fiancé had witnessed secret meetings of *farrapo* chiefs in back rooms of Reading Centers, aboard ships. They'd planned a combined land and sea operation on their town, in fact General Davi Canabarro and Colonel Nuñes were already on the march. But Captain Garibaldi's gunboats were trapped way to the south in the Lagoon of the Ducks. The fiancé had heard that the foreign sailor had the death penalty hanging over his head in Italy, in Rio de Janeiro had started up Rio Grande's navy with 12 men and one ship, and had been tortured in Gualeguay, Argentina, hung by the wrists from a roof beam, by governor Leonardo Millan. Rumor had it that Garibaldi had transported his *lanchas,* gunboats, over land to Lake Tramandai, which connected to the Atlantic. Armed rebels in place in Laguna had their stations to take when they saw Rio Grande's cavalry or flotilla approaching. Maria da Gloria and her fiancé supplied guns.

Her village changed. Young men disappeared from taverns and cafes, old men laughed at the sight of a national guardsman. Two hundred national guardsmen finally occupied Laguna, mingling as spies among the citizenry of 20,000, manning three imperial men-of-war and the fort protecting Laguna from naval attack.

She knew they were on the front lines when she passed the

well-appointed, make-shift hospital and Dr. Fortunata came out looking pale, fatigued. He asked for help.

Wounded soldiers spilled into the hallway, onto the veranda. She fed them, gave them drink, dressed wounds. She searched the faces of the bodies brought in for her husband's. She consoled the dying, squeezing hands, a warm word. They called her by the names of lost loved ones, some called her *"mamãe"*. She contacted the gravediggers.

Fall passed to winter. In Henrique's house she cooked up stews with pumpkin and manioc, fetched water. She glanced out the window at the waters below, the high ridge across the treacherous channel. She stayed up nights, watching, waiting. One night it rained. Another night a dense fog engulfed the harbor. The moon passed through its phases. July 21 waned without a sign of troop movements on the ridge or vessels below. She fell asleep.

5. NIGHT MOVES

Captain José Garibaldi was in the river, shoving the gunboat *Seival* with about 30 hands.

The night before, General Canabarro had ordered 100 men under Garibaldi to board the *Seival* in order to pave the way for the cavalry charges, marines acting as vanguard for ground forces. Garibaldi had taken the helm from the local pilot Juan Enriques, but then the *Seival* ran aground on a reef and Garibaldi ordered the marines, 30 hands, into the water.

Now they pushed, urged on by Garibaldi calling their names. He directed angling of the poles worked by the sailors aboard. There were also horses on board. The helm moved a few palms. In unison the men pushed, maneuvered--another palm of movement and the gunboat released.

Garibaldi bounded to the helm. The *Seival* sailed up river.

Then Garibaldi was ordered to take command of an infantry detachment two miles away. Strategy against superior forces was to attack simultaneously from different directions. The North American Quaker John Griggs took the *Seival's* helm. Garibaldi and a small detachment swam to the riverbank, holding on to their horses' manes, tails. They were to move at daybreak but the imperial flotilla, as Garibaldi had predicted, was active during the night, so he positioned his men along the riverbank.

Around daybreak, the imperial warships *Itaparica* and *Lagunense* opened fire on Teixeira Nunes' cavalry approaching from the south. Then, as if it was an apparition, some sort of ghost ship, a gunboat flying Rio Grande's red, green and yellow, approached from the southwest.

The *Seival* was on Lake Garopera. How could she have gotten there? The crown's intelligence was the same as Maria da Glória's--the Republican flotilla was trapped way to the south in the Lagoon of the Ducks. On the Lagoon's northeast shore lay the deep Capivari Bay-- here Captain Garibaldi had drawn up his gunboats the *Seival* and *Rio Pardo*, then he contacted local shipwright Joaquim de Abreu, who built eight solid wooden wheels connected by steel axles. Garibaldi and his marines lifted the gunboats in the water, placed the wheels underneath until the keels lay on the axles in such a way as to not interfere with the wheels' free action. The marines rounded up 200 draught oxen, attached strong towlines boats to oxen. The oxen were urged to pull, they pulled--and the gunboats emerged gradually from the water and began sailing across the plain to Lake Tramandai 54 miles away, which connected to the Atlantic.

The imperial warship *Catarinense* sailed upriver to attract the *Seival* to the furious mouth, where the *Lagunense* waited. John Griggs retreated, then opened fire with his two bronze cannon, alerting the *farrapo* camps. General Canabarro ordered the general attack. Teixeira Nuñes' cavalry poured over the ridge, down onto the imperial fort. From the riverbank, Garibaldi and his infantry opened a murderous fire on the *Catarinense*. Her crew set her on fire. John Griggs, holding his wooden stick, boarded the *Lagunense*. Her crew abandoned without a fight. In the panic, loyalist colonel Vilas Boas ordered a mass retreat. Hot-blooded Colonel Nuñes flew after them.

6. OCCUPATION AMID CHEERS

She awoke to gunshots, screams, bombs exploding. Her first thoughts were about whether the *farrapos* had committed atrocities against the people, as her husband had said they would. She ran out past the orange and mango groves, down the jagged path through bushes, tall canes and bougainvillea. In the main plaza she found the intense confusion of retreating imperial troops. Nothing had happened to the people, no one had harmed them.

Wild, beautiful Maria da Glória led the forces of Castilhos and Nunes into the plaza, then grabbed the flag in Castilhos' hand and led the cheering crowd down to the beach. Women greeted the landing marines and decorated their swords with flowers.

General Canabarro, an Islander, declared that day, July 22, National Day. Church bells pealed. Women decorated windows, doorways and the Town Hall with red, green and yellow ribbons they'd hand stitched. At night, torchlights lit the front of buildings.

Next day a "*Te Deum*" was said in *Sant'Antonio dos Anjos* of white marble and gilded altarpiece. She entered the church for the first time since her marriage and stood in the rear.

The gaucho chiefs huddled around the altar. Heavy, smoking a cigar, General Canabarro and Teixeira Nunes who never lost a battle-- they were dark, with high cheekbones, wearing *vinchas*, or headbands; open-throat shirts with the national red, green and yellow knotted around their necks; long, cotton, lace-trimmed drawers and over these, pulled around the waist, a large square of hand-woven cloth called *"chiripa,"* "against the wind"; wide cowhide belts held together with silver plaques; narrow brim, black felt hats with chin strap; shoes made from the tubular section of a horse's hind legs, the hock making a natural heel; The Italian Luigi Rossetti, Rio Grande's Secretary of State; Captain Massimo, leader of the Black Lancers, part of the infantry: tall, in a blue poncho, holding an 18-foot bamboo spear twin-tipped with steel crescent and spike. Weapons also included pistol, carbine, bayonet, poncho-buckler and *façon* stuck in back of the belt, used in addition to killing to cutting the throats of cattle and skinning them, paring rawhide thongs, plaiting saddles, mending gear, slicing off slabs of meat from the carcass and picking the teeth; The foreign sailor Garibaldi.

People around her whispered he was the one who'd taken the ships in the capture of their port. He was very tan. In the light of the candles his reddish-brown beard shined like gold.

7. *SAUDADE,* or the SADNESS of PARTING

She smiled out at Captain Garibaldi from her window, around noon, as he paced the quarterdeck of the captured topsail schooner *Itaparika* of seven guns, anchored close to the hill. The hill rose sharply from the beach, dwarfing the schooner and her captain.

Hips rolling, legs bowed, shined black leather boots tic-ticking along wooden boards, Garibaldi paced with his troubled eyes, fair brows knit, down on the quarterdeck, oblivious to the beauty of surrounding nature: sky and water one dark blue, long-beaked blackbirds swirling overhead, Laguna surrounded on three sides by mountains--marriage of mountain and sea, terraces bearing fruit and flowers, houses nestled into ancient rock; and the highway of scents, salt and tar drifting up on balmy sea breezes, olives and hydrangeas cascading down.

Garibaldi was about 32 years old. He wore a gray poncho, blue trousers, black beret, black silk scarf around his neck he drew up to protect his ears from the morning dew and his face when the sun was high. His chestnut hair, falling well below his shoulders, fired in the sunlight. High, narrow waist together with wide hips made a belt unnecessary but he wore a sash to hold his telescope, pistol, long knife. Sheathed saber balanced easily on his left shoulder.

Four warships, 14 merchant vessels captured and sixteen cannon, 500 guns, 36,000 packs of bullets. Seventeen imperialists killed, one *farrapo*. Seventy-seven prisoners taken, including one officer who'd had a choice of dying or coming over. But it wouldn't have mattered how the war was going--Garibaldi was desperate.

The shipwreck only a few weeks ago had taken the lives of 16 out of 30, and all the Italians had gone down. Of his friends who'd made those desolate shores like home, not one was left: Mutru, Carniglia, Staderini, Navone, Giovanni D.--all carried westward by the currents and buried in the coastal sands without stones to mark their bones.

His desperation and attempts to reason through them those winter days in late July 1839 began with the idea of marriage. He owned too independent a nature, was drawn invariably to a life of adventure to have ever considered marriage. But in the immense void left by the shipwreck--so sudden, horrible--he felt the need of a human heart he could keep near him always. He went on to think how he'd always felt the need of a friend. The survivors were valiant men but still strangers. He'd found his good friend Luigi Rossetti again but couldn't live with him, saw him about once a week, as Rossetti was busy with affairs of state and his paper *O Povo*, The People. Then--a woman! A woman would love him and live with him. Women were the most perfect of god's creatures and whatever men might say, it was easier to find a loving heart among women than among men. Unless he found a woman to love him and live with him, and that immediately, his life would be insupportable.

He was feeling a word found only in the Portuguese, *saudade*. *Saudade* is the sadness one feels on parting. Seafaring men experience *saudade*--the way a ship leaves port, slowly; the way faces on piers, shores, fall away slowly. And there was something magical about Garibaldi's ships and it had to do with women. Sight of his first ship, for example, the *Costanza*--his mother upstairs readying his bags, crying; Peppino, as he was called, outside looking toward the harbor and the *Costanza* came to him as if in a magical dream, transformed to a luscious young woman: figurehead on the bowsprit *pettorutto*, high-breasted; sides ample; masting lofty, light; deck spacious and clear.

Garibaldi withdrew his wooden telescope, trained it on the hill. Low, simple houses cascaded up. In such a house near the summit, for the past two days around noon, a young woman smiled out at him.

Her admiration was clear, transparent. In her smile he'd been seeing the vitality and tenderness some knowledge of him aroused in her--death penalty hanging over his head in Italy, here he was in South America; started up Rio Grande's navy with 12 men and one ship while the empire had 67 warships carrying 2,830 men, one steamship, 350 guns; captured and tortured, hung by his wrists from a roof beam, in Gualeguay, Argentina, and survived; it was he, as the people around her said, who'd taken the hostile ships in the capture of their port.

Today she wasn't at her window.

Quickly, Garibaldi tracked to the flowering trees nearby, then out to a clearing with small fountain. Young women filled their pails and pitchers. One attracted his attention above the others. He focused until she filled his small, round glass.

Her appearance possessed *una bellezza irregolare*, an unusual stark beauty reminiscent of Frida Kahlo, a beauty outside the ordinariness of the lady-like norm. So powerful was the impression she made on him that he ordered the dinghy put down. He rowed furiously to shore, beached his craft, then sliced up through the bushes and tall canes.

She wasn't at the fountain.

Through the flowering trees he rushed, his heart pounding, up to a terrace dotted with houses. He searched one, another under the guise of billeting troops. He was about to give up hope when someone called him--Henrique, the shopkeeper he'd met on first entering the town. Henrique invited him home for coffee.

She'd been working outside and it was cold, about 40 degrees, though the flowers were always in bloom. She wore a blue cotton blouse open at the neck, sleeves to the elbows, full green skirt, low leather shoes and a *lenço*, scarf, of green cloth. She heard Henrique speaking to someone at the door, turned. Standing in front of her was Captain José Garibaldi.

They remained silent, enraptured.

He was the kind of man, Garibaldi described himself, who preferred storms to the calms and doldrums of the heart--lightning flashed and in the sheer, scalding light they shared the presentiment they'd met before, sought in one another's face something that made it easier to recall the forgotten past and found it, a kind of miracle, at the same time giving birth to romantic love and sibling connection--a present, living exuberance and solacing; aged silence that spoke of companionship, loyalty, playfulness of children; of faces, voices, images of respective pasts so disparate yet familiar, mutually understood.

To Garibaldi she looked strong, healthy. She'd used her body. He recognized her maturity coupled with charm. In her eyes, in the beautiful glow of her dark face, he saw she could give him what he needed.

She was agitated, too. She was feeling *saudade*, too.

Garibaldi could speak *Portuñol*, combination Spanish-Portuguese. Instead, he blurted out in Italian, language of the country he dreamed of building: "*Devi esser mia!* You must be mine!"

8. FROM TEMPEST TO CALM

Anita & Jose at that time

Garibaldi didn't pick her up and, whether she acquiesced or kicked her legs, carry her off to his ship. He would write that from this moment on Anita accompanied him on all his adventures--but they didn't ship out until late October. He left out the moments between late July and October, when Laguna's own Jaboticabeiras began to bear fruit, rose bushes their flowers.

Captain Garibaldi must have gotten a response. She gave him one.

In the split-second needed for it, his own fateful words reverberated around his body like the strings of the *cantor's* guitar sounding madly and beautifully inside an armadillo's carapace, the wandering minstrel's box. His words etched themselves in his heart and mind, and echoed, and would echo until the end of his days with the force and clarity of the first wild stallion he saw on the vast, virgin plains of Uruguay.

His first words to her forged a bond that only death could break. But she was alive now and took the vow in silence, looking straight into his eyes. She understood more from his eyes than his pronouncement or booming tenor voice. His fired eyes had listened to the dictates of his heart, and she knew something about love. His eyes spoke of a man in war, of horrible loss, which she also knew. And they were citizens--citizens were soldiers of the Republican army. Any further display of emotion wasn't necessary. She turned and ran up the stairs, holding her skirt, to Henrique's wife, Miguela, then the women prepared coffee in the kitchen set apart.

From the beginning, she had a way with Garibaldi. She ushered him gently from tempest to calm and merged with him as on the long, uneventful voyage: cool, with iron nerve. Her human heart's first reaction acted as a kind of anchor he'd never dropped before--rooting, at the same time allowing all sails to fill and his ship to glide into the open sea against strong headwinds. Garibaldi preferred country life to city life its fragrances, sounds, silences. He could relax now and have that proffered cup of coffee.

What a beginning to an afternoon coffee! Henrique must have thought. He followed her lead, too, the easy, wise way she allowed the afternoon to go on, allowing Henrique his nature of citizen of the South, hospitable, generous--in Nature's abundance the land and its products, including coffee, were gifts to all.

One of Henrique's great pleasures was the aroma of coffee filling his house. His wife and their friend Aninha carried in the coffee.

On the great *estancias*, small farms and *charqueadas*, meat-salting plants, serially interdependent landowners, peons, Blacks and Indians ate at the same table often under the stars. Hands passed around the *maté* gourd and lips sipped from the same *bambilla,* straw. During wartime, home for all were primitive huts and tents. Women made and pitched tents, unfolding them from their saddlebags. Women cared for spare horses, disciplined children. Women had to be strong and pleasing. She and Miguela pleased Henrique and their guest by making good, strong coffee. Since she was on the periphery of Henrique's family, she pleased by showing good manners and listening--while Captain Garibaldi spoke, she didn't take her eyes from him. He thanked the women with a courteous nod. In a tone corresponding to the courtesy of his movements, his eyes penetrating and pensive, mild and friendly, muscles around his eyes pursed from sailing into hard gales, Garibaldi mentioned the campaign's beginning was brilliant, bold. Outnumbered almost two to one, they had to fight a defensive war that embraced surprise offensive strikes, like their initial incursion into Santa Catarina and Colonel Nuñes' pursuit of Vilas Boas to Destêrro. A tough defense had to be mounted in order to hold, give time, for Republican principles to triumph. The warchief put the citizen-soldiers' minds at ease as far as atrocities against the people.

"General Canabarro is a brave and honest soldier, a little rough but kind-hearted, and he devised all sorts of fine projects."

The export tax on *charque,* meat, had already been reduced. And a provincial presidential election had been scheduled--one candidate was Father Vincente F. dos Santos Cordeiro. Influential priest, they all agreed, hopefully also among coffee growers, who in effect ran the empire.

Garibaldi stood up, nodding in politeness to the women. He invited them to come aboard the flagship. Then he walked to the door with his slow, heavy tread, accompanied by Henrique. She joined the men at the door. Garibaldi offered his hand. She clasped it as his equal. She watched him on his way awhile, his steps quickening, until he disappeared into the flowering trees.

She looked at her palm. She could still feel his hand, hear the strange pronunciation of his tender voice.

9. COURTSHIP UNDER FIRE

The fiery pitch of love at first sight was too violent, too fleeting, too short a tallow for Garibaldi to have ravished her straightaway, so she couldn't have desired to ravish him, couldn't have compensated for abuse at the hands of men, save for her father, by making love right away to a man she desired that way, opening the mollusk as a way of salving his desperation and redirecting her aborted, abused desire--her sighs drifting up from the caches nature provided: bushes, tall canes and secluded stretch of beach on the far side of the hill, into the salt air and black night sky. They had to have time to make sure of their love, so they basked awhile in love's spring sun.

Garibaldi awaited his next order. In the meantime, they conducted a wartime courtship, one reflecting their life together as it turned out: hazardous, painful, lighthearted, always true.

Three imperial men-of-war blocked food and other essentials from coming in, ships from getting out. But the hostile ships weren't equipped for navigating shallow water with shoals, so Garibaldi had time to set up defenses against a naval attack. He posted a battery of one small-caliber cannon on the eastern point, outfitted captured merchant vessels with 7-pounder swivels placed amidships, repaired the 20 ships of his squadron. Lacking in resources, he had to rely on manpower. Townsfolk built launches and carried matériel, bolts of canvas, coils of rigging. The sound and echo of hammers were heard all around.

Another Republican vessel was added when the 14-ton *Caçapava* entered Laguna overland on wheels. That was a sight to go and see.

Garibaldi rarely left his ships, going ashore once a week to meet with General Canabarro and Luigi Rossetti. The captain returned at dusk and issued the next day's assignments with affection and a smile, not lacking in authority. Every day around noon he raised his black silk scarf, wiped his brow, looked up--she was at her window, smiling out at him. Now in place of his desperation and her quiet wisdom, they shared the secret of their unspoken love.

But the entire world appeared to know, stand between them.

Garibaldi bumped into Henrique again, in the good shopkeeper's eyes saw his admiration of her. Then a cloud passed over Henrique's face and he told Garibaldi she was married, not knowing the Italian was playing according to rules of medieval courtly love whereby the object of veneration *must* be married and there *must* be a romantic element of danger, jealous husband's fury, spiteful talebearers.

The faint reds of sunrise filtered through the hospital windows onto her as she searched the bodies brought in more desperately now. Her life couldn't go on unless she knew her husband's fate. Sweating, hands trembling, she was feeding a one-arm soldier whose other arm was in a sling when suddenly his eyes widened, lit up, and he looked beyond her, knocking over her spoon. "*Viva!*"

"*Viva!*" the other soldiers shouted in unison.

She didn't have to turn, look toward the door.

At the door, Captain Garibaldi spread his arms slightly in receipt of the salutations. He tried to direct attention away from himself to their nurse, nodding in her direction.

She pressed Miguela to arrange a visit to the flagship.

Garibaldi assigned John Griggs the task of showing the guests around the *Itaparica* of seven guns. Tall, gaunt, face narrow and chiseled, the North American Quaker received with good humor his mates' jokes over how he would fight just with a wooden stick. The stone Garibaldi would rest on Griggs' scattered remains spoke of an excellent sailor and shipwright, Griggs having built the shipwrecked *Rio Pardo* from the wood of the forest along the Comaquã River, forging the iron from the very nails to the masts' iron rings; of a young man of admirable courage, charming character. When a letter came from his relations in the United States, announcing he'd succeeded to an enormous fortune, asking him to return home, John Griggs had already met with a glorious death.

He guided the guests to the forward part of the topsail schooner, pointed up. They looked up at majestic fore and aft sails, masts of equal height. The rigging was standing and running--standing rigging permanent, supporting the masts; running rigging those lines controlling the sails' shape.

She'd never been on a ship, such a ship. She leaned over the bow and followed the anchor line down to the water--calm bed somehow holding up this 12-ton sea-home.

John Griggs showed them to stools on the weather side. They watched the sunset.

Around the same age, 18, and loving the same man, she and Griggs became friends.

Godmother, good friend of the mother, she held the baby boy in her arms in *Sant'Antonio dos Anjos'* sacristy. She edged away from the altar, glanced at the muted blues fracturing through stained glass. The men, as usual, were late.

Leather boots tick-ticked along the marble floor--godfather and father, Garibaldi and one of his sailors. The child was baptized "Edoardo," after Edoardo Mutru, the captain's boyhood friend who'd drowned in the Araranguà River.

Somewhere--in hospital, aboard ship--she and José made arrangements to meet alone.

Midnight, foggy midnight, she waited in the bushes of the narrow trail climbing to a cabin on top used by shepherds in springtime. Branches crackled--she lost her breath, stretched out her arms, found José. They burrowed up the hill a ways, snapping off branches. José stopped. His rosy lips overgrown with chestnut hair murmured into her hair the color of night.

"I love you too much, mustn't have you."

"Why? I love you." She clung to him as if to a life-raft.

"My heart is with you but my destiny is where other men await me. Promise to meet me here tomorrow night."

Of course she promised.

General Davi Canabarro's headquarters were in the Capuchin monastery, outskirts of town. Candles burned and flickered, monks said evening vespers. One monk served the general his *asado*, assortment of roast meat. Luigi Rossetti worked at the general's side.

The general tended to isolate himself, brood over what would happen when sacrifice was required of the people. At times his mood swung to optimism, like on the Town Hall steps after the *"Te Deum"*-- she was in the crowd--and the general pronounced: "A Hydra will arise from the lagoon to devour the empire!"

His shifting moods reflected his dilemma--liberating a town or region through military force, then, according to Rio Grande's seat of government in Piratini, set up and maintain an administration adopting the rights and guarantees assured by the government from which they'd seceded. Canabarro was to be guided by the principles of civil power, military command a delegated function, and always remember the revolution proclaimed solidarity with Benjamin Costant's democratic principle: "In no society founded on the sovereignty of the people can any individual or class subject the rest to his or its will."

We're reluctant to continue, tending to stay close to her, afraid if we leave momentarily, she'll be gone forever.

What the people of Rio Grande wanted for themselves, essentially local rights and franchises, they wanted for the people of the other Brazilian provinces. National unity was to be re-established through the ideas of the French Revolution, Declaration of Independence in Philadelphia and *Giovine Italia,* Young Italy. Common bonds of nationality--history, politics, economics, folklore, journalism, theater--took precedence over regional life. The fate of their vision, one nation under a Republican regime, was really in the hands of citizen-patriots who mustn't give up their right of expression, thinking for themselves.

Four days after taking Laguna, General Canabarro named municipal assemblymen to act as interim government. They declared Laguna capital of the new independent province. But assemblymen couldn't make a decision without first consulting the military command. The general ordered confiscation of all public sites, assets and estates of citizens who'd fled. Luigi Rosseti, always at the general's side--"He was made for this kind of thing," Garibaldi wrote of his friend--warned of their haughty bearing against the good people of Catarina and reminded the general that the true capital, where enemy troops were concentrated, was still Desterro. Canabarro's immediate plan became taking of the capital, and he occupied himself with troop movements, territorial expansion--as his Azorean ancestors had done.

This is what the general was doing between July and October, onset of spring.

Rossetti set the date for the provincial presidential election. The two candidates put forward were Father Vincente Cordeiro, as we know, and his nephew Joachim Xavier de Neves.

The election was a fiasco, can make us laugh.

Neves' reputation was of a revolutionary, exalted liberal--but when the fighting started he went into hiding in the town of San José, at the same time accepting from loyalist governor Pardal the task of stopping Teixiera Nunes' advance. General Canabarro nominated Neves *coronel,* commander of forces that should invade Desterro. Nuñes sent Neves the order to stop Vilas Boas' retreat. Neves did nothing to defend San José against Nuñes, also refused to arrest Canabarro's emissary who came to tell him Rio Grande was counting on him. Neves informed the crown about what was going on, requested troops to resist Teixeira Nunes.

Governor Pardal, furious at Neves' sitting on the fence, refused the request, instead ordered San José's forts demolished and its artillery buried. San José's Justice of the Peace, Caldeira de Andrade, tried to arrest Canabarro's emissary but failed. At least Andrade's action was decisive--Governor Pardal sent Andrade reinforcements.

Of all people Governor Pardal stuck out like a sore thumb all the way to Rio de Janeiro. The governor was replaced by a naval squadron under Admiral Frederico Mariath and a land army under Marshal José de Sousa Soares Andréia--who, she and Maria da Glória knew, had wiped out the Black Guard of Para along the Amazon.

Meanwhile, 22 voters went to the polls. Of 21 votes counted, one apparently lost, four were for Padre Cordeiro, 17 for Joachim Neves.

General Andréia embraced the new president. "Neves, my colleague, salutations from the regent in the name of his Majesty the emperor [King Dom Pedro II, nine years old]." Dumbfounded, Neves stared at Andréia. "I now inform you that you are accountable with your life for any insurrection in the capital. Or you can accept your new assignment in the German settlement of San Leopoldo."

Neves went to San Leopoldo, never to be heard from again. Padre Cordeiro replaced his nephew as provincial president of Santa Catarina.

A new song was sung across the land:

Un abraço do regente
(A hug from the regent)
Faz virar num momento
(Produces turncoats instantly).

General Canabarro felt humiliated, worried about his reputation in Rio Grande--his present mood. His original decision not to accept the expedition into Santa Catarina appeared correct. The general gave the warchiefs their new orders.

10. THE AGONY OF HAPPINESS

Garibaldi's order was to clear the coast of enemy ships. He needed a night move to get through the line of imperial men-of-war blocking access to the sea. The second major issue facing him now was whether she should go with him. Her fate was always in men's hands.

It became known as Garibaldean to take up a good cause at the point it appeared lost. Her cause was clearly lost. If her husband was killed, she would spend the rest of her days a widow without children, nothing. If Duarte survived the war, she would spend the rest of her life with the wrong man, a brutal wrong man, continuing as object of disgrace and, recently, of vilification, being openly called "*putan,*" even traitor. Her cause was good because she was good and he loved her, admired and respected her, needed her as much as she needed him. His life without her now would be even more insupportable than his life without a woman to live with him and love him following the shipwreck. His desperation had taken on character, human life--it was she.

She had to meet José at her workplace, the fountain, be captured where he'd first seen her--in the small, round circle of his glass. She must suffer, be tormented, pay dearly for her freedom.

Drawing water, she noticed a band of *Tangaras*, singing and dancing redbirds, alight in a line on a nearby branch. Waiting for the *Tangara mestre* to set the others dancing, she sang softly a popular song of the day:

I go into the open air where there's grass and no people,
And I'm free to sigh.
The pain I feel inside keeps growing.

If I add my pain to the bird's tender chanting,
I silence it.
And my pain keeps growing.

Her cresting pain was pierced by slow, heavy footsteps--José's.

He lifted his left high-top black boot onto the stone base and relaxed, powerful body arching back, poncho and beret draped over his right arm, free arm reaching out, ready to cup her words.

She wore a long, white, short-sleeve cotton dress hanging loosely, Grecian folds catching the moon's rays. She stood on the fountain base as on a throne, looming magisterially over him, projecting white-with-some-shadow against the shadows of giant *taquara* [bamboo] leaves blooming behind, her arms folded across her chest as on a corpse or caressing something or someone invisible and precious.

A beam of moonlight separated them.

"Do you see the redbirds? We call them 'The Dancers,' they fly together, obeying one leader--it's rare you actually see them dance."

He would be leaving Laguna soon.

She pretended to faint, then laughed and buoyed herself up. Knowing what the evil tongues were saying, he wanted to leave her.

They would be drawn into combat. She would become a homeless wanderer, an exile. In other words, she would become just like him.

"I can offer the free open sky as a roof, hunger in the stomach, clothes in shreds, instant death any moment and, as single compensation, a free and generous heart to give to the fatherland." Then a steely fire came into his eyes. "Cross with your own feet that beam of moonlight between your prison and my ship."

She summoned all her strength. Her legs were leaden.

Who remembered that Duarte was the one who'd left? And he never truly was her husband, between them there was nothing at all, not tenderness or a smile or any common interest.

She took a step...

A woman had to pay for everything, even her own suffering, and had to be silent and good, kneel in front of the altar and thank god for breathing and being able to wash dirty clothes.

She stepped into the heart of the moonbeam...

She had the guts to show her love with purity and loyalty, rejecting the hypocrisy habitually imposed on women--if a woman lives with a man who has one or more lovers, she's respected; but if she loves one man without documents, she's condemned. She loved José more than anyone, anything in the world...

She hurried across the outer edge of moonlight and jumped into his waiting arms and smile.

Arm-in-arm they climbed the hill's western slope to the cabin on top used by shepherds in springtime. She felt cold, shivered. He lifted and arranged her shawl around her shoulders.

The last shepherds had prepared a fire for the first to return.

Dogwood and a mound of hay lay in one corner. She kindled the wood with a long wooden match. The wood burned fast. José gathered the straw, piled it before the fire.

How must a man love her?

In his kisses she felt his strength, the warm gentleness of his desire. They made love till flame was cinder.

11. COMBAT AT SEA

Laguna's own Jaboticabeiras bore fruit, rose bushes their flowers. Spring had come.

The dense fog engulfing the harbor during the entire day of October 23 promised blackness, silence of night. Moon, harbor lights and torchlights in front of the houses wouldn't illuminate the mission's three ships: *Seival* commanded by Lorenzo Natal, *Caçapava* by John Griggs, *Rio Pardo* by Garibaldi. He'd renamed a captured merchant vessel after the original.

Over the next two weeks she would achieve fame in Rio Grande.

She waited on the beach, wicker bag beside her. Gray fog rolled over her face. On the way down she'd given her sewing scissors to Maria da Gloria, who then passed into the glory of her history. Out of the fog came José's dinghy.

She jumped in.

José rowed the way the Indian propelled his canoe--barely immersing the short, light paddle that resembled a marine animal's foot, stroking forward, backward, right to left. The course was straight, balanced; the advance slow, silent, invisible.

She climbed up the *Rio Pardo's* ladder first. Her first step aboard she became the first active female combatant in Rio Grande's navy. As their war was about full integration into the Brazilian empire, she may have been the first active female combatant in any nation's navy.

Captain Garibaldi introduced her to the officers: "May I present my wife, Anita Garibaldi."

The crew, about 40 hands, was made up of local recruits, freed negroes and *frères de la cote*, seafaring adventurers. Garibaldi explained in French his method of disciplining the troops: "*Je lui brule la cervelle, main cela n'arrive que rarement.* I blow out the brains but that occurs only rarely."

The officers bowed to her.

How wonderful, what a privilege to see her love in his element! José jumped around like an acrobat, issued orders in a voice she hadn't heard before--like a trumpet. Sails took wind, filling, flapping. She looked up--the *Rio Pardo* began sailing out.

Her honeymoon cabin was small, narrow, low ceiling.

"Please don't say it's a good excuse for staying in our bunk."

She has to question the new name, Anita, he'd given to her up on deck. "Anita" has carried down 150 years.

"Aninha is the diminutive. In Italy we call the woman 'Anita'. From the first time I saw you, you were the woman."

She played at being child-like. "Anita! Anita! Oh, I like it! It's harsher but I like it!"

His men didn't know their destination until they got there. Garibaldi told *her*, only *her*, ten years he told her. They were sailing for Quemadas, small harbor in Republican hands. As for his night move, how they got through the blockade line--yesterday he'd leaked information that the *Caçapava* was sailing south on a mission, then last night John Griggs sailed her north, weapons displayed, and the three men-of-war followed. The *Rio Pardo* was sailing in their wake, toward Quemadas.

Up on deck, wind slapped on sails and waves crashed into wood. Two sailors kept the nightwatch.

She and José bathed one another, washed and combed one another's hair. Seen from behind, they were man and man, woman and woman--her skin dark, his rosy; her hair slightly longer and black, his reddish-brown.

Awaking alone, she put on a pair of José's leggings and rolled them up. She went up on deck A shower of sunlight greeted her, the sea a bed of near-blinding, dancing silver.

Sailors showed her knots, how to loosen and hurl the grappling irons, use the signal flags, level and fire the 7-pounder swivel amidships. She was a gay, interested student.

A shot rang out.

She was told to hit the deck, gun close to her chest. She followed orders.

A sharpshooting contest was held--seagulls.

Her *Tio Antonio* had taught her never to miss a target. She took aim, the ship swerved sharply, she fired and missed. She fired again, this time at a compensating angle, and hit the gull.

She saluted Rio Grande's flag. She turned with a look of pride to José.

His look was serious, somber. She adopted the same serious, somber look.

The *Rio Pardo* continued sailing north, penetrating waters outside Saó Paulo, one day's sail from Rio de Janeiro--deepest penetration Rio Grande's armed forces made into the crown's heartland. She was a most threatening *farrapo*.

They met up with an imperial corvette which pursued them in vain two days. She learned the difference between a capable commander and an inept one. If the corvette had had a capable commander, the poor, little *Rio Pardo* would have been knocked to pieces, as she had one 9-pounder swivel while the corvette had 20 large guns in a covered battery. The commander was so inept they threatened to board. The corvette opened fire with her 20 guns.

"Go below!" José's eyes shined, as if he was about to kiss her.

The sailor next to her was hit, fell. She summoned assistance and carried him out of danger.

A heavy southern squall put an end to combat. Next day they kept close to shore. She set up a first-aid station.

Near the isle of Abrigo, they approached a *sumaca* close enough to board. A *sumaca* was a fast, twin-masted man-of-war with square mainsails. She hurled a grappling iron--it soared, fixed. She swung in with 20 sailors and the captain. The *sumaca's* crew surrendered without a fight--but in that split-second when hand-to-hand fighting was still an option, she realized her greatest weapon: she was the sole woman among fighting men, and at the point the enemy in front of her understood this, when she violently swung her hair from her face, he froze, terrified, giving her that split-second to wound or kill.

The *sumaca* was laden with rice. Garibaldi assigned a pilot and prize crew.

They captured a brig John Griggs had already plundered. Griggs had placed a few men aboard but they were attacked, put in irons. It was a stroke of good luck that friends fell in their way.

On their eighth day out, Garibaldi received the order to return to Laguna.

José liked to tell her that luck, good or bad, often came in pairs--the order must be an exception. He poured over maps, reports. She could tell when something was up, not by his edginess or pacing, but by the way he suddenly looked away, that faraway look coming over his face. The person with him, beginning with his mother, wondered what he was thinking about.

They would not fare well on the run back to Laguna. Before they left, the people had begun to show them ill-will. Lack of diplomacy and their own stupidity had alienated the people, as Rossetti warned. General Andréia was taking advantage by marching toward Laguna on the double with four cavalry squadrons and 2,000 foot soldiers.

With a strong breeze astern, the *Rio Pardo* made sail for Laguna.

Near the island Santa Catarina, about 20 miles from Laguna, the forward lookout spotted a *patacho,* kind of brig-schooner. Garibaldi fixed the *Adurinha* in his glass. She was cruising eastward close as possible to the wind off her port quarter, starboard gunwale mostly underwater. The sea was running high. She was going to notify the men-of-war off Santa Catarina of their movements.

"Attack!"

Without wasting a second, long enough for her to catch her breath, the captain signaled John Griggs with flags to make for "Im-bi-tu-ba," Republican stronghold.

John Griggs aboard the *Caçapava* made sail for Imbituba.

The *Seival*, Captain Lorenzo Natal, had been lost during a moonless night.

Garibaldi steered the *Rio Pardo* within musket fire of the *Adurinha*, luffed sharply to port.

"Fire cannon, muskets!" The crew opened fire.

The *patacho* replied with her seven guns, blowing holes in the *Rio Pardo's* sails. The *Seival's* cannon was dismantled, she sprung a leak. The captain of their prize with rice struck colors, was running to shore. Garibaldi responded: "He's lost his presence of mind."

The northeasterly veering to south, it was impossible to reach Laguna. They followed John Griggs to Imbituba, anchoring close to shore.

The *Andurinha* notified the men-of-war off Santa Catarina of their movements. The *Rio Pardo's* crew prepared for combat.

She sewed up the holes in their sails. Instead of remounting the *Caçapava's* cannon, in the first darkness, she helped carry the cannon up the hill on the bay's eastern point. She snapped off branches and carried wood in building a *parapetto gabbionato*, a hidden gallery with breastworks for the cannoneer, stalwart Manuel Rodriguez.

At daybreak, three enemy men-of-war approached.

When outnumbered, Garibaldi usually attacked. He sailed out the *Rio Pardo*, close enough to use carbines--the reason for attacking. Garibaldi maneuvered in such a way that the enemy ships got caught between the *Rio Pardo* and Manuel Rodriguez' hidden gallery.

She looked toward the bridge...

José was commanding from there, knife and pistol in his sash, her green scarf tied around his head. Then she saw something strange, incredible--José was smiling and saluting. Before a battle, her love smiled and saluted.

Seaward-blowing winds favored the imperial vessels. They were able to tack about while directing a murderous fire, riddling the *Rio Pardo's* flanks with holes; she became like a sieve. Corpses covered the deck. Garibaldi resolved to fight to the death, his resolve strengthened "by the imposing sight of my Brazilian wife who not only disdained to be put ashore, but took part in the glorious battle, gun in hand."

Manuel Rodriguez fired well-aimed shots from the hill on the eastern point.

Amid continuous deafening explosions, bullets whizzing and raining down, the enemy attacking from two sides, their crew jumping from one side of the *Rio Pardo* to the other, screaming, she was taken over by a kind of stupor. "Attack! Attack!" she screamed.

From the bridge covered with blood and mutilated bodies, José looked for her. "Go down! Go down!"

A ball hit nearby. She went down onto two dead bodies.

José sprung to her.

Dizzy, she got up. "I'm all right. I'm all right."

"Go below..."

"I'm going but to get the cowards hiding down there."

She went below. A few minutes later she came up again, leading out a few men at swordpoint.

At the point there was no longer any hope, enemy vessels sheared off. A trick, the captain said. They'll resume attack under cover of night.

She spent the rest of the day caring for the wounded. The dead were buried at sea without stones to mark their bones.

Night fell but the enemy didn't return. The *Bella Americana's* commander had been killed.

In the silent, black night, they climbed up the hill for the *Caçapava's* faithful cannon, carried it back down and shipped it.

South wind falling to calm, protected by darkness, they weighed anchor for Laguna. Enemy ships noticed their departure and fired a few shots. By then the *Rio Pardo* was already some distance away.

12. DEFEND AND RETREAT

Their friends received them with joy. The military command was at a loss to explain how they'd escaped so superior a force, at a loss to explain her--great horsewoman, like them, a bit queerly, woman gaucho--how could she give up land for water, horse for ship? A gaucho losing his horse under any circumstance was a disgrace. Water was an obstacle to movement, boat a prison. Saxon colonialists possessed the instincts of the sailor. But what sailor could receive a tiger alone, dagger in hand, rolled up poncho in the other, dagger thrust into the tiger's mouth while his heart was transfixed? She was held up as a hero.

The *Rio Pardo's* glorious encounters, together with the crown's loss of 7,000 troops thus far, established the Republicans as extremely dangerous. But instead of taking advantage, the commanders engaged in personal quarrels. Treason, the sin of venality, was born in a commander's heart. It appeared the entire expedition had been undertaken with insufficient means because of reciprocal jealousies. People all over the province rose against the weak Republican government--loyalty to the crown, that is, "turning," inspired by fear. "Fear," wrote the ancient Roman Petronius, "was invented by the gods." The imperial god of fear then was Marshal Soares Andréia.

He "pacified" town after town by waistcoating, sewing up revolutionaries in rawhide sacks, then dumping them in fields, prey to carrion crows; tossing young men's heads into halls where their families danced; shooting the paralyzed and blind; imposing contributions on women whose husbands, fathers, sons were absent; forcing women to cook, whipping those who refused.

She and José lived aboard the *Rio Pardo*. She prepared the wounded, transported them to hospital on horse-drawn wooden carts. There was no news of Manuel Duarte.

Imaruy, a small fishing village 10 miles north of Laguna, had turned. General Canabarro ordered Garibaldi to retake Imaruy and sack it as a way of teaching the people a lesson.

Garibaldi believed violence only bred more violence. Canabarro ordered him to obey or resign.

The mission filled him with such anguish, such embarrassment that José couldn't share it with her.

Evil talebearers were driving him away.

Thirty-two imperial warships were on their way to Laguna. They'd arrive in conjunction with General Andréia's land army approaching on the double in a wide semi-circle. Canabarro was vain, hesitated. He believed he could stand up to Andréia. Retreat was inevitable very soon. José needed her there, in Laguna, to round up with John Griggs as many small crafts they could borrow or steal. They would need the boats for transport.

A farewell to Maria Bento is needed.

She climbed the hill against the blazing sunset to Henrique's low, simple house, surrounded by orange and mango groves. Good Henrique opened the door, stepped aside. Maria Bento had come to take her back to Carniça. The pirate had raped her and carried her off, people were saying. She was a disgrace to her family and to the women of Brazil.

She did not see her mother and sisters again.

Imaruy's garrison, all locals, was on the lakeside. Garibaldi landed three miles beyond with 30 new awkward, eager recruits and as many horses. At night, 30 horses galloped off the *Seival* into shallow water. The nocturnal attack came from the mountainside.

Imaruy's garrison retreated in wild flight.

Inhabitants of the nearby hills drew their supplies from Imaruy, so the town was well-stocked with stores of all kinds, especially wines and liquors. The new recruits looted the wine shops first. Within the hour there was general drunkenness. Imaruy went up in flames.

Mounted, sword drawn, Garibaldi threatened, shoved and even cut down a few of his own men. He was unable to stop devastation to property. By morning, small fires burned, and the town was empty. Garibaldi loaded provisions, three casks of brandy for the division. A German sergeant was killed, and Garibaldi ordered him buried on the spot. The new recruits wanted to take the body back to Laguna for honorable burial.

She waited for José on the Rio Pardo. He came home. He would write:

"I wish for myself and everyone else who hasn't ceased to be human that he may never be in a situation of being ordered to sack. It's impossible to describe the atrociousness, meanness. The authority of my command was powerless against the unleashed lust to rape, rob. Of no effect was the threat that the enemy was returning in double strength. Fifty could have overwhelmed us. The men wanted to take back a German sergeant's body. I noticed a light in the hold, approached and looked down. The men were shooting dice, playing table the German sergeant's chest. He'd been a tall, stout man. Candles stuck in bottles circled the body. In the light of the candles the men looked like demons playing for souls."

She consoled José.

Early the next morning, preparations began for retreat. There was so little time for her.

Garibaldi was placed in charge of transporting their entire division to the right bank of the *barra*, bar of the harbor. The number of men was small, mainly cavalry of many horses and baggage.

She and John Griggs showed the captain the small crafts they had gathered, lined up along the shore. First horses, munitions, arms and supplies; then men and their families were ferried across the narrow, treacherous channel. Currents near the lagoon's exit was strong and wide, and could hardly be avoided without getting too near the coast. Garibaldi positioned his flotilla along the right bank to provide cover. The captain placed her in charge of the *Rio Pardo*.

When she got relief, she rowed the dinghy to the beach. She regrouped mounted squadrons and foot divisions, organized women and children. Their sole escape was over the high ridge across the waterway. Throughout the morning until high noon, she glimpsed José at the wharves, instructing the boatmen; steering across the channel; on the hill.

Through his telescope Garibaldi saw Admiral Mariath's 22 imperial warships, crowded with troops. The vessels of no great draught were suited to the water's depth at the lagoon's entrance. Landside, General Andréia's cavalry and infantry approached on the double. Part of Garibaldi's eye captured the beauty of the rich summer landscape fed by the rainy spring season--exuberant forests; great expanse of land producing rice, mandioca, maize, wheat and hemp; the inlet itself was beautiful, surrounded on four sides by mountains. Inhabitants were fleeing, looting shops on their way out. Houses left open were being robbed. First of the imperial vessels entered the lagoon. Garibaldi rode down the hill, jumped in his dinghy, rowed furiously to the *Rio Pardo*.

She'd already fired the first cannon shot. Her words reanimated the men's flagging spirits. They fired small arms. Griggs aboard the *Seival* and local pilot Juan Henriques aboard the *Itaparica* echoed her shot with their own, inflicting heavy damage.

The *Rio Pardo's* cannon was wrecked. She reached for a musket and fired, not once seeking protection of the bulkhead, not once bending down.

Admiral Mariath's entire squadron entered the lagoon, favoring northeasterly and the tide redoubling their speed. They anchored within artillery and small arms fire. Bombardment was incessant, rigorous. The waterway through which they'd passed was narrow. Retreat was taking place at a distance of 150 paces.

Go to Canabarro and ask for reinforcements, José ordered her. Infantry properly placed could wreak havoc. And she was to stay ashore, send the reply with an officer they could trust.

She returned herself with the general's order--set fire to the fleet and retreat to shore with all they could save. She implemented the order on the *Rio Pardo*, José on the *Seival* and *Itaparica*.

The enemy continued to rake them.

She made trip after trip, transporting wounded, weapons and munitions.

Garibaldi stepped aboard the *Seival* and walked over busts separated from bodies, each step contacting dismembered limbs. He touched the bodies, feeling for heartbeats. Juan Enriques had a hole in his chest large enough to pass an arm, his body surrounded by two-thirds of his crew. The rest carried the wounded into launches, tried to load arms and munitions. Garibaldi spread brandy from a cask taken in Imaruy.

The *Itaparika* was a shambles. From below, his vision clouded by smoke, Garibaldi saw John Griggs standing on the far side of the deck against the bulwarks. "Abandon ship!"

Griggs didn't respond, didn't move.

Garibaldi made his way to him. Griggs' eyes were open, the look on his face serene, fair complexion unchanged. His trunk was pinned to the bulwarks with grapeshot, the bottom of his body scattered all around. He'd been blown to the opposite side of the flagship from where he was standing, struck by grapeshot in such a way, at such close range, that the whole lower part of his body was carried away. Garibaldi looked away.

She stood erect in the dinghy's poop, calm and proud, like a statue of Pallas Athene. José trembled in fear for her. She'd made 20 journeys to and fro, each under heavy fire, in a dinghy rowed by two men whose heads were ducked all the time.

She and José spread brandy on the *Rio Pardo,* lit matches in least flammable places, then ran. The *Rio Pardo* went up in flames. They did the same aboard the *Seival* and *Itaparica*--lit matches, tossed them and ran.

It was night. She and José stood on the beach at the foot of the wooded ridge, surrounded by the wounded, horses, munitions and baggage. The wood of the ships burned, smoke thick, black and acrid with burning flesh.

At least their brave dead had a worthy burial place, reduced to ashes on decks of their own ships.

John Griggs, Quaker--he'd built the original *Rio Pardo.* She was a queen among schooners, all copper inside, masts strengthened with iron, rudder obedient as the tail of a bird. She had such a beautiful shape, like a swan.

13. GARIBALDI'S TREASURE

She was in her element now, land and horses. She was more at ease on horseback than the Italians, José and Luigi Rossetti. She rode vanguard with Teixeira Nuñes, leading 80 survivors south along the beachline. Waves hammered the coast, could be heard miles inland. Even the distant sierra seemed to tremble. Wind off the ocean was so strong it was called "carpenter of the beach". Her face showed her exhilaration, shining, unnerved by the ocean spray glancing off her face. The tendency was to veer inland, away from the violent sea--but her course was straight and balanced, like the Indian propelling his canoe. Content with taking Laguna, General Andréia wasn't pursuing. They could ride with some ease now, inland, west toward the mountains. By morning they reached a lake fed by mountain streams and encamped.

The wounded were cared for. Unlike the imperial army, the *farrapos* didn't have a surgeon--cold compresses, herbs. The more seriously wounded asked to be killed, and were. Women unfolded tents from their saddlebags, raised them. A typical tent was a piece of rawhide stretched across four lances. Gauchos rode out for food. Women cared for the spare horses, feeding and watering them. Soon the gauchos drove in a small herd of wild cattle. They were killed, bled, skinned with amazing speed and dexterity. Beef quarters were roasted vertically on green branches so juices could cascade down.

Women and children ate first. She asked José to eat with him.

What could he say? When women describe her, most often she's lighthearted, even funny, somewhat obsequious. Around the campfire, women poured *maté*. Hands passed around the warm gourd, lips sipped from the same *bambilla*. Eyes turned mechanically toward the faintest whisper in the dry grass, into the distance in search of sinister visages and to the horses within firelight, whether their ears were pricked.

People of the mountain district Cima da Serra were about to be overrun by a superior force and asked General Canabarro for help. She and Rossetti looked toward Teixiera Nuñes, whose land this was, too. The decision was made to go to the mountain peoples' aid.

Later on, all asleep save for a few sentinels, puffs of white clouds drifting across the black sky of a million stars, she lay stretched across José's lap by the lake.

"Now I know why I came to South America." An amnesty lifting his death penalty in Italy had been unlikely. His merchant captain's license, second grade, had been revoked. He had wished to travel further afield than the Aegean and Black Seas. South America's climate was more congenial than the havens of Switzerland and London with their frost and snow, dampness and rain. José looked away. She has to be prepared to go to Italy. "I came to learn how to fight. I'll take back to Italy the very essence of what animates these men. I'll take back a style of war France has forgotten and Austria cannot even imagine." He caressed her hair. "We'll walk among the lemon trees of the Riviera, color of old gold, leaves bright green."

She turned up her face. In her eyes he saw the shine of the stars. Arms around waists, they went into their tent. A moment later, half-naked, she came out holding her sword and stuck it in the ground beside their tent. In the early morning sunshine, she and José washed their clothes in the lake and dried them on rocks. Naked, they waded into the water. José swam like a fish. She played at being helpless, laughed. They rollicked together in the water.

The small band was ready to ride. She sidemounted, no saddle. Her unbraided hair fell to her waist, bodice bright green again. She smiled at José and he at her.

"Anita was my treasure and no less zealous for the sacred cause of nations and a life of adventure. She looked upon battles as a pleasure and the hardships of camp life as a pastime. So that, however things turned out, the future smiled on us, and the vast American deserts unrolling before our eyes were all the more delightful and beautiful for their wildness."

Her immediate future was the 450-mile ride to the mountains across the vast, undulating American plains. She saw for the first time herds of wild stallions, prancing ostriches, loping antelopes, moody bulls. Up ahead the forested mountains looked blue and the pine trees colossal--columns mighty enough to uphold the vault of heaven.

She reached the foot of the mountains. Pine trees towered over her, dwarfing her. She and majority of the others had never been in the great mountain forest called the "backbone of Brazil" because it stretched from the Rio de la Plata's alluvial flats to those of the Amazon. Pulling goats, mules and cattle, they began the climb. To save breath, they didn't sing.

The terrain was like a dried-up riverbed, good walking for the goats but the horses kept sliding. There was no path. She hacked her way through with her long knife. Decayed stalks and leaves of giant *taquara* plants piled up among the pines, forming a virtually impassable soft moss that acted like quicksand.

Pulling their mules and goats, José looked up at the piece of heaven between pine tops. She wasn't beside him. He backtracked to her.

"You should have told me you were tired."

"I wanted you to come back and carry me."

José picked her up. "You weigh no more than those bits of clouds."

Further up, the fog grew dense. She and José heard a roar-- waterfall spilling a rainbow. They stopped and made a fire.

"She" remembered as "they"--memory not confined to the literate of the two. They would remember this time, isolated from the others, the air perfumed with pine cones. "Ah, resin and pine..."

After five days, they picked up the *picada,* or path, leading to Cima da Serra. This mountain district together with Lajes and Vacaria formed a triangular clearing in the forest--their theater of war the next 18 months.

They affected a junction with the *Serrãos*, people of Cima da

Serra.

On December 14 ('39), five months after she had to be his, she saw her first guerrilla action on land.

Imperial General Francisco da Cunha crossed the Pelotas River with 500 cavalry, intending to head off the Republicans' advance. Acunha camped in a stone corral with the sign, *Santa Vitória*.

She stood in perfect blackness, total silence. Even their horses didn't move. Their attack was so sudden and so swift, it froze her, whirled her horse around. Battle order was infantry first, corps of Black Lancers attacking on foot. The Lancers are remembered:

"The courageous freedmen, proud of their task, drew up in solid order and seemed a perfect forest of lances. This incomparable corps was composed of negro slaves liberated by the Republic and chosen from among the best horsebreakers in the province. Their lances beyond the ordinary length of 10 feet, their coal-black faces, their sturdy limbs hardened by constant and vigorous exercise and their perfect discipline struck terror into the foe."

The Black Lancers pushed the imperial cavalry to the edge of the Pelotas River, then in. She saw José faintly, sword in hand riding up and down the line of infantry firing from the riverbank. She dismounted, rushed to the side of a wounded soldier, then another. She whistled, horses came. With a few men she carried the wounded from the field. She saw General Acunha hit in the middle of the Pelotas River and use his last ounce to remain mounted, then piece by piece, slowly, collapse into the river.

The imperial soldiers retreated.

Garibaldi would call their first child "Child of Victory" because he was conceived in the aftermath of the Battle of Santa Vitória. Here, now is that aftermath...

She knelt beside an imperial soldier's body, along the riverbank. She tried to read something on a ribbon pinned to his uniform. Out of the corner of her eye, amid the fog rolling in, she recognized José's boots standing beside her, caked now with mud and blood.

"What does this ribbon say?"

Silence.

"José, what does this ribbon say?"

When he didn't respond this time, she looked up. José was panting and sweating, screwed up face caked with mud, heavy cavalry sword in his hand bent and covered with blood. He threw off his sword, dropped beside her. She opened her arms. They made love on the riverbank in the dense, rolling fog.

Lieutenant Basilio who'd turned for money was brought before Colonel Nuñes. Without taking his cigar out of his mouth, the colonel blew out the turncoat's brains.

14. SHADOWS OF MEMORY

She carried Rio Grande's flag through the mountain districts of Vaccaria, Cima da Serra. Then the triumphant Republicans entered Lajes.

She is shadow. Her memory is shadow.

She rode into Lajes slowly, José beside her. They came to a shadow across the road. She stopped, José stopped. The shadow was cast by a large, wild fig tree overhanging a stone garden wall. She guided her horse around the shadow, José following.

Her sisters had been born in Lajes, her mother had told her, right on the road to the Sorocoba meat markets up north, this road. A wild fig tree climbed over the wall around the house, the tree so big it cast its shadow across the road.

She and José quartered in a small cabin with pine roof and bed, fine new surface to break in. They spent a few peaceful days sheltered from the elements.

The first in a long procession of local women came to pay her homage. The women of Lajes brought her a muslin dress, leather shoes, green silk scarf. She was gracious and shy, just like José. She made a dessert with prune sauce.

Imperial Colonel Antônio de Mello Albuquerque had increased his cavalry by 500, raising hopes of the imperial party. Mello turned his forces toward São Paulo for fresh horses, linen. But Colonel Nuñes didn't know whether Mello was coming by way of Vacaria or

Curitibanos, so the colonel decided to divide his forces--Colonel Aranha taking the Serrão cavalry to Vacaria, Nunes himself marching with part of the cavalry and Garibaldi's infantry to Curitibanos.

Garibaldi believed that in their position, with all forces, they could not only oppose Mello, but utterly rout him. But it was a time in his life when he was not only learning to love, but utterly taking orders. They despised the enemy too much, Garibaldi felt. She witnessed his feeling.

She asked to take charge of munitions. When asked why, she answered, "So that they'll be served out well."

She changed out of her muslin dress and into leather, her new leather shoes and fit her hair into the crown of her hat and draped her new green shawl over her shoulders. She mounted beside José, rode out with the cavalry made up of prisoners taken at Santa Vitória. Seen from afar, except for her green shawl, she was one of the men.

They marched three days deep into the highlands, on the eve of the third day reached the Marombas Pass. They encamped.

During the night a few shots rang out from the outposts. From that moment on until daybreak, they stood ready for action, quiet and still. The night passed, its sounds and colors changing, moon arcing across the brightening sky.

At dawn's first light, Colonel Mello with 400 cavalry and 100 national guardsmen drew up in a long line on top of a hill, deep valley in front overgrown with thick bushes. The Republicans had 200.

She was astonished by the enemy's superior numbers.

Nunes had to send word to Colonel Aranha to join them--but the hot-blooded colonel who had never lost a battle was afraid of losing the opportunity for a fight. Nunes drew and pointed his sword toward Garibaldi--"Attack!"

Garibaldi's detachment of infantry charged out in skirmishing order. His sable hair rose and fell as he ran, then he and his men hid behind bushes in the valley and opened fire.

She rode back to the supply of munitions.

Colonel Mello retreated--a feint. Garibaldi pursued, after crossing the deep valley was charged in flank by Mello's hidden cavalry. Garibaldi retreated to the main body.

Teixeira Nunes saw Manuel N., one of his best officers, killed.

Garibaldi's column reinforced, they marched forward.

Mello retreated again, a real retreat, leaving one dead in the field--one dead appeared like a real retreat. Mello and his forces slipped out of sight.

Major Jacinto reported to Colonel Nunes that Mello's *ganado* and *cavalhadas* were crossing the Curitibanos River. *Ganado* was a herd of cattle driven along for the supply of the army; *cavalhadas,* spare horses.

Nunes and his cavalry set off at a gallop. The greatest horsemen in the world passed Garibaldi and his infantry, who tried to keep up.

Colonel Mello had driven his cattle and spare horses across the river--but again hid cavalry detachments behind the hills.

Nunes fell into the ambush. His flank was annihilated and scattered by detachments of flying, shooting, slashing, *bolas*-hurling cavalry. The great gaucho Nunes lost his first battle.

She was about to create a story true and a legend that Garibaldi would tell around campfires the remainder of his days.

She stayed behind with the baggage train, galloping up and down hills. Firing in the distance told her that soon munitions would be exhausted. She urged forward the supply of munitions.

Mello's cavalry in pursuit of Nuñes' flying cavalry came across her and other soldiers of the baggage train. She spotted an opening for escape, instead called on the men to fight. Putting spurs to her horse, drawing her long knife, with a vigorous spring she charged into the midst of attacking cavalry. They shot at her. One bullet passed through her hat, grazing her skull, carrying away locks of hair. Blinded by smoke and dust, amid the deafening clamor, she found herself isolated. Then she found herself surrounded. A *bolas*' three stone balls and rawhide wrapped around her horse's legs, he went down. She went down with him, rolling, scraping and bleeding.

Sunset witnessed the field covered with dead bodies.

She was brought into Colonel Mello's tent lit by candles, her clothes torn and blood-stained. Ah, a woman! staff officers marveled, and they marveled at her courage, yet did not possess the good taste to conceal, in the presence of a woman, their pride in their victory; they expressed contempt for the beaten Republicans. She responded with rough, disdainful pride of her own, fighting as vigorously with her tongue as with her weapons.

She was shown a plain woolen poncho--José's. He'd been killed, she was told. She asked to bury him where he'd fallen. Mello agreed. A staff sergeant lead her out to the battlefield.

It was as it had been, covered with dead bodies, except night had set in, moon sharp and bright. The sergeant's face moved in and out of lantern light. She pulled his sleeve, stopping him, and captured his face in full light. He was Gonçalves Padilha, the gallant sergeant who'd asked for her hand in Laguna and had appealed to godfather Braga, who told him she was promised to another.

She and Padilha wandered like shades over the blood-soaked plain. She turned over men who'd fallen face down who by reason of their clothes and figure bore resemblance to José. Moonlight flashed on faces of the dead who weren't Garibaldi. Her actions quickened as fewer and fewer bodies remained. José wasn't among the dead.

He'd escaped into the forest with 73 men and posted sentinels to watch for her. As night wore on, he grew more and more anxious--by ten o'clock was half-crazed. The enemy began to pursue. One of his men accidentally fired his gun, scattering horses and some men. And José had wounded, including Major Jacinto. Now he'd had no choice but to retreat to Lajes.

Not finding José's body gave her the courage to escape. On the way back to the stockade, she took in the surrounding countryside, in the light of the moon spotted a farmhouse roof peeking up from a clump of trees. The stockade held 12 men, a section set off just for her.

The guards drank, didn't watch her. On the third night of drinking and not watching, she slipped out, covered by a poncho. She ran to the farmhouse, knocked. Two old women, sisters, opened the door.

She was a woman in need of help...

The sisters looked her up and down, glanced at one another in disbelief. The person at the door wasn't a woman, unless the world had created a type they'd not as yet seen.

Quickly, flipping up her poncho, she tore open her bodice, revealing full breasts. She was a woman.

Women were angels in situations of this kind, José had told her. The two old sisters were angels, preparing a bath, cooking, washing, mending, fresh linen. They gave her a pair of breeches, military coat, boots and a new hat. They gave her a spirited horse. She set out at daybreak.

She rode through tropical forests swarming with jaguars, pumas, tigers. She leapt over rocks during a rainstorm--lightning flashing, thunder clapping. She walked and talked to her horse. Four days they ate berries, soft green shoots. She crossed 50 miles of desert and yellow wasteland without water. She flew through hostile pickets, fords of rivers. The Canoas River was swollen with rains, doubled by mountain streams. She swam 500 yards, holding on to her horse's mane.

On the opposite bank a few loyalists lay in ambush. Seeing her pull herself up on her horse, swiftly take off her hat so that long black hair fell around her face, then her dark face staring at them--the ambushers turned and ran. Later on they testified they'd been "pursued by a mysterious being."

She came to a ridge. Down below a few riders galloped into Lajes, José's long golden hair flowing behind.

He thought she was dead. She thought he was dead, too. She asked for a cup of coffee.

15. GUERILLA CHIEF

Only the Canoas River separated the Republicans from the imperialists. She'd had some experience with that river. They couldn't hold or defend the Canoas with 70-odd men.

When Garibaldi and his 73 men returned to Lajes, wealthy merchants had already established the imperial form of government. Then, after two successive defeats, the cold growing intolerable, lacking food and suitable clothing, Republican soldiers deserted, taking their own horses and more.

Garibaldi was ordered to descend the sierra with his infantry, Nuñes to follow with cavalry--all to join the main army at Malacara.

Her and José's division, 60 in number, began the descent. Narrow, enclosed on both sides by impenetrable thickets, the *Pelufo picada* cut through the thickest part of the jungle. Mountaineers surrounded them and pounced on them, raging, shouting and pursued with rifle shots. These natives of the country made more noise than possessed skill. One horse was killed, a few men wounded. Finally, the Republicans reached headquarters in Malacara, 12 miles from Pôrto Alegre.

She lived in a rustic hut, southern bank of the Lagoon of the Ducks. Here, stomach well swollen, she spoke with Rio Grande's president Bento Gonçalves da Silva about Rio Grande's heart and soul, which, 50 years later, 1888, became the foundation of the Brazilian

Republic.

She was sewing. José was at the window, singing. A horse...

Elegantly mounted against last stained reds of sunset, in high, shiny, leather riding boots, hair silver and groomed, the president approached a beautiful tenor voice, faint at first, drifting out over the lagoon. Bento entered the doorless hut.

She handed the great gaucho a *maté*. Sipping the warm, familiar, bitter tea, Bento mused:

"In the beginning, in Rio, it was so easy to recognize us with our straw hats, green jackets, flowers in the lapel. It was very Republican to wear a cheap hat, eat Westphalia ham and turtle soup at Maseri's coffee shop. But we really were inflamed, devoted to liberty and the Republic. On the morning of September 27, '35, when my troops crossed the Azena Bridge, they carried the Brazilian flag. Red is the color of the moment, cry of alert. We'll always be lead by things that touch our hearts."

Their next action was an attack on San José do Norte. The fortified town had an abundance of food, arms, munitions, and was the sole harbor in the province--they shouldn't have to depend on Montevideo for connection to the ocean. San José was also the *atalaya*, the signal mast indicating the water's depth to ships. Six hundred loyalists occupied the fort-town. The Republicans were attacking with twice that number. President Bento Gonçalves told her she wasn't going. "A little absence is good for love." She was seven months' pregnant.

According to Garibaldi, Bento Gonçalves was "a venerable, noble warrior but he lacked stubborn endurance and was unlucky in battle."

No matter how José tried to explain, she was going with him to San José.

She was cavalry chief seven months' pregnant.

She rode with 1,200 men, silent, under a tempestuous downpour. An uninterrupted march of eight days, at no less than 25 miles per day, exposed to heavy rains and cold winds, brought them unexpectedly to the fort-town's walls. It was a night in July, one of those wintry nights when shelter and a little bit of fire were gifts from heaven.

"Who goes there?" was the signal for attack. Wrapping their miserable rags around them, she and the men prepared for the attack.

She commanded a cavalry detachment guarding the officers' horses.

The men crept up to the well-manned walls.

"Who goes there?"

The Republicans opened fire. The sentinels went down.

Climbing on shoulders, they entered the fort-town. One hour later they were masters of the trenches and three of four forts. But the Republican soldiers--hungry, in rags--drank, ate and plundered. Drunken soldiers lined up 20 prisoners, executed four, the fifth a boy of 12. Garibaldi stopped the execution.

"The boy might yet be able to render good service to the

community."

The imperialists recovered from the surprise, massing to several hundred.

Garibaldi and other commanders rushed around, seeking men to renew the attack. But they were drunk, loaded with booty, muskets damaged from battering in doors and shops.

San José had been built on the lake's edge. Imperial men-of-war began raking the streets.

When reinforcements didn't come, Garibaldi summoned her and her cavalry. She stormed through the gate, gun in hand, charged into soldiers looting and assembled their broken ranks.

During the night the Black Lancers had taken the largest fort, *Imperial*, occupying a commanding position in the center of line of trenches. It wasn't yet light when a tremendous store of gunpowder exploded, blowing up the fort. Clothes on fire, the Lancers went flying through the air like glowworms and crashed to the ground horribly mutilated.

The devastated Republican army retreated around noon. Her cavalry detachment covered the retreat.

16. MENOTTI, CHILD OF VICTORY

She rode from the disaster of São José with a skeleton of division, 40 men, north 100 miles to the town of São Simão--a desolate sandy waste flooded by rains. José found an *estância* abandoned by the Count of São Simão in a wide, beautiful valley, with cattle for food, water and large supply of horses. Their mission was to collect canoes for the next campaign and establish communication with the other side of the lake.

No canoes came their way. They gentled wild colts. Captain Máximo and remaining Black Lancers took tame horses to nearby Roça Velha for safeguarding.

One-arm, fierce imperial guerrilla Moringue raided Republican troop units scattered throughout the territory. He'd lost an arm in the Battle of 14 against 150, Edoardo Mutru fighting and John Griggs with his wooden stick. Moringue's method was to transport troops by water, land them, reinforce with cavalry. He scattered enemy horses by tying dried hides to the tails of wild ponies then driving them into the corral--the noise of flapping hides scattering the horses. The great guerrilla took no hostages, only superior horses, then transported them to the crown's base in Pôrto Alegre. Moringue raided the farm in São Simão.

Defending unarmed, she fell hard from her horse. Her attackers were killed by a few men who rushed up.

José persuaded her to go to a tranquil farm in Mostardos, run by midwife Maria Costa who had four children of her own.

September 14, 1841, she gave birth to a boy--dark complexion, deep scar on his forehead.

The father: "A child of victory, conceived in the aftermath of the Battle of Santa Vitória. His mother's serious fall from her horse inflicted a scar on the infant's head."

She and José named him "Menotti," after the Modenese patriot Ciro Menotti, hung on a public gibbet after writing to his wife, Cecchina: "When my children grow up, let them know how well I loved my country."

She and Menotti lacked warm clothes, linen. They had no money. José decided to go to Setembrina to friends who would lend some, Luigi Rossetti. She watched José ride out a ways. Fields of alluvial soil flooded, he rode through water up to his horse's belly.

Garibaldi arrived in Roça Velha during a violent rainstorm, welcomed by Captain Máximo, rain driving onto reserve horses in the corrals. The storm raged into morning. Captain Máximo urged Garibaldi to stay--but his mission was too important.

After a few miles, Garibaldi heard shots coming from the Black Lancers' farm, hesitated but kept going. In Setembrina, Garibaldi and Rossetti bought warm clothes, linen, needles, threads and a large handkerchief of many colors.

Rossetti had seen her in action in São José do Norte. "She's an amalgam of two elemental forces, the charm and tenderness of a woman, symbolized by the daring and vigor with which she brandished her sword, and the beautiful oval of her face that trimmed the softness of her extraordinary eyes."

Garibaldi made Rossetti promise to tell her himself, ushering Rossetti to a glorious death.

Garibaldi passed back through Roça Velha. The rain had stopped, the sun shining on Captain Máximo, 30 Black Lancers and the weaker horses dead around the farm.

Garibaldi rode hard to São Simão. He didn't find his family where he'd left them. "Anita! What has become of Anita!" He entered the nearby forest and called, called her name--it sounded, echoed among the trees. He came to a fork, hesitated then went deeper into the forest, still calling.

In a dreadful storm, half-clad, she had mounted a horse and, with her son set across the saddlebow, had taken refuge in the forest. She ran out, holding 12-day-old Menotti.

17. DISASTROUS RETREAT

She and José with Menotti transferred quarters to the left bank of the Capivari River. They built two canoes and ferried persons, baggage, mail along the Lagoon of the Ducks' western shore.

She was a ferrywoman.

A coup d'état in Rio de Janeiro produced a change in government, offering amnesty and measure of home rule in return for surrender. At the same time, a fresh army under General Caxias, supposed best general to appear thus far on both sides, was on the march to the South.

Bento Gonçalves da Silva refused the terms for himself. The President's decision and hers and José's were the same. The better part of the army also refused, creating bad feelings among the rest who, like the people, were tired of the fighting.

She, holding Menotti, José and their division began the difficult retreat through the forest of the *Antas*, their mission to clear the mountain passes of General Labattue. Bento Gonçalves and his forces followed, covering Garibaldi's movements. Luigi Rossetti and his corps of clerks were the last to march.

Moringue surprised them. Rossetti fell, gravely wounded, from his horse. He replied to calls of surrender with sword strokes, was run through and rolled dead under the belly of his fallen horse.

The weight on her heart over Rossetti's loss is not spoken or written.

She and their division retreated through gorges and forest, under rain falling in torrents, driving along a few haltered cows; no other provisions could be transported on the precipitous mountain paths.

She held Menotti, José pulled along a few dozen mules and horses, some for riding, some for carrying baggage. José had seen the *Antas'* hide, never the animal itself--like an ass, wild, harmless, flesh exquisite. Rivers running high in flood rolled over men, arms, baggage. Most of the baggage was carried away. The column camped under the same conditions--soaked, hungry. In the interval between one torrent and the next, those whose turn it was to stay with the cows had some food. They could hardly get *taquara* leaves for use as fodder. The cavalry killed horses for food but didn't share with the infantry. She marched with Menotti in the rain without food. Other women and children fell behind, dead or dying of hunger and cold. Cavalry picked up some of the children. Most of the younger children died.

She feared losing Menotti. In the steepest part of the track, while crossing torrents, she carried her son slung from her neck in the large, colorful handkerchief Rossetti had bought, and kept him warm with her breath.

Bugrès Indians didn't cover their *fogas*, deep pits, with earth, and didn't attack from stockades of logs along the path. Instead, the *Bugrès* attacked and slaughtered General Labattue and his men.

Then the guides lost the way.

Of her and José's 12 mules and horses, four were left. One of them riding two horses might get into open country, find food. Carrying Menotti, she rode ahead. José labored to save the exhausted mules, cutting sedge and bamboo. He had to abandon the mules. Famished, he set out alone, on foot. She reached the end of the forest's path. A few soldiers were warming themselves around a fire. Quickly they dried some rags, wrapped them around half-frozen Menotti, went off and found food.

After a long search, José found her and Menotti. They left the forest.

Immediately, as if the brutal conditions of the past nine days were confined to the forest, they encountered beautiful weather, found cattle, and the fruits *guava* and *arassà*. In Vaccaria they awaited Bento Gonçalves' division, who then arrived in groups in terrible condition, untiring Moringue having attacked them, giving General Labattue time to reach the imperial army. But Labattue's troops had deserted after attacks by the Bugrés.

She marched slowly now, they weren't being pursued. Lacking horses, the remaining Black Lancers captured horses and gentled them. After wandering through the forests *Portughez* and *Castellano,* they arrived in Cruz Alta--a small, well-built town on a plateau of pleasant surroundings. Soldiers erected barracks. José built a hut. As was her custom, before going to sleep she came out half-naked and stuck her sword in the ground beside their hut.

At this time she and José heard about an Italian in San Gabriel, Francesco Anzani. Like so many, Mr. Anzani had been exiled from

Italy, then he fought in France on the fifth of June '32, in Oporto during the long siege and in the war in Portugal, going by "Ferrari." Anzani had risen to the rank of captain for his valor and received two wounds--one in the head, one in the chest. Now he was chief assistant--cashier, bookkeeper, confidential clerk--to two merchants in São Gabriel. The forest close by served as refuge to the Bugrès Indians, one chief making himself terror of the town. Anzani confronted and beat up the chief, who never showed himself in São Gabriel again.

José went to São Gabriel to meet this Anzani. From a distance he saw a man stripped to the waist washing a shirt and trousers in the stream.

"Mr. Anzani, I'm Giuseppe Garibaldi."

They talked about the war. It was just about over, they agreed. The next morning Mr. Anzani was gone, leaving behind one of his two shirts.

José told her about Francesco Anzani.

She and José decided to go to Montevideo. "At least for a time," they told Bento Gonçalves. José's last six years had been filled with dangers, hardships, no news of his family back in Nice. Most of all, Menotti needed a safer place. Not a word about her hardships and her family, lost forever now. Bento gave them a herd of cattle in payment for their service to Rio Grande.

She and José worked hard several days rounding up 900 head in the *Curral das Pedras*. Behold a *tropeiro!* She was a herder!

The drive to Montevideo was 400 miles. There were no trails, the land dusty and dry. The rivers were swollen and there were swamps. Menotti rode in a small, pony-driven cart, protected from bumps by ponchos and blankets wrapped around him. With the settling in of the black night, she pointed up. Menotti looked up at the Southern Cross, Three Marias, forever dying Diamond of Venus.

Every day after counting the herd, José made a fire. She cooked the meal of the day, most often *passoca*, dried meat with dried beans mixed with mandioca, a root ground into flower. Soon they lacked food, fodder. They tried to sell worn-out cows, at times receiving one half-dollar. Half the herd drowned crossing the Rio Negro River, the remaining head exhausted. With help from a farmer on the Uruguayan border, she and José skinned 300 head for hides, then bundled and strapped the hides to their horses.

They rode another 200 miles. On the fiftieth day they arrived in Montevideo, capital city of the Republic of Uruguay.

PART II: URUGUAY (1841-48)

18. MONTEVIDEO, BIG CITY

She rode in slowly, holding Menotti. She'd never seen or even been in such a vibrant, cosmopolitan city, citizens of all kinds side by side: Spanish, Portuguese, French, Basque, Italian; palaces beside slums; narrow streets jammed with traffic opening into spacious parks; food markets sprawling near magnificent white beaches; and elegant women of high society and diplomatic circles parading in fancy silk dresses and bonnets, carrying parasols, their eyes gaping at José.

As the world grew larger, as Garibaldi approached his dream, there's less about her. She supported Garibaldi days, months and years, seven in all, in Montevideo, often alone in the worn-torn capital, poor and her pantry half-empty.

Now, from her horse, she looked up and around. Like Laguna and Nice, Montevideo was surrounded by water--on the south by the open sea, west and north by the harbor. Across the bay to the west stood the hill-fort *El Cerro*.

José didn't need to go undercover--a successful coup had changed the government. Like all new citizens entering Montevideo, she, José and Menotti reported to the police.

"José Garibalde with wife and one son arrived in Montevideo from San Gabriel on June 17, 1841."

They went around to hide merchants for the best price. She negotiated, José wasn't good at business. She had a way of running her hand over surfaces she held precious--José's face, mosaics, fabric, now the hides captured her imagination. No one knew what was in her mind and heart. She ran her hand slowly over the hides. The best she could do wasn't enough to finance a place. They stayed with José's friends, Napoleone Castellini, wealthy shipbuilder, and his wife, Mariquita.

José took a job as salesman of grains, cheeses, European fabrics. Carrying samples, he went door-to-door, to commercial houses with a band in one corner and lovely, young French girls as *commesse*, salesgirls. José was serious about presentation, running his hand over the finest silk only four *reales* per yard. Soon they had enough to finance a place.

She went apartment hunting with Menotti, straight to the harbor district, the city's poorest. She looked at a gray rowhouse, a share, on Calle Porton . It had a gaslight directly in front, bars on the windows; inside a front parlor, bedroom, family room with stone floor; and an oven out back, outhouse. A flight of stone steps lead to a roof terrace looking out over the harbor. She took it.

She, Menotti, José settled into civilian life. In the evenings, still some daylight, she and José played with Menotti. José read local and European newspapers and she sewed. They went to sleep at the end of daylight, no tent, no ground to stick her sword into.

Friends visited: Giambattista Cuneo, called "*Il Credente,*" the Believer, who owned his own newspaper; Castellani, Giovanni Risso. She lit candles, prepared and served *maté*.

Uruguay was in a state of civil war, internal discords caused by rival claims of two generals, Manuel Oribe and Fructuoso Rivera. After several victories, Rivera ousted Oribe and seized power. Oribe fled to Argentina where Dictator Manuel de Rosas welcomed him and employed him against the Unitarians. Rosas' party was the Federalists. Party affiliations notwithstanding, Rosas was a despot, rural caudillo run amok in the sophisticated capital city Buenos Aires. Dictator Rosas wanted Uruguay, had gone to war to get it.

Cuneo tried to interest his old friend, fellow Young Italian, in the war. José was a salesman now.

But it was a brutal war. Traveling with each Argentine battalion was a *degollador*, cutthroat, who passed down the line of prisoners holding a special knife with curved blade, placed his free arm around the prisoner's neck and whispered: "A woman suffers more in childbirth"--then slit the throat. And Rosistas mutilated corpses.

José wasn't interested in civil war.

But the war had international repercussions, France and England with trading interests in the Plata region, diplomatic missions in Montevideo and Buenos Aires. The war was being covered by papers in Europe, United States.

On one of his selling rounds, José passed a shipyard and went in. Ships were being sold at very low prices and timbers broken up, bundled and sold. The ships had cost the republic enormous sums, properly developed could establish Uruguay's preeminence on the Rio de la Plata.

Orders from Minister of War Francesco Vidal, the shipworkers told Garibaldi. Vidal had declared the navy a burden to the state.

A sailor who'd been with them in Laguna stopped José on the street, asked for money to buy a shirt for his new job.

"I already had a job. My shirt wasn't indispensable to me."

As for his own job--if another salesman couldn't sell ice in summertime, how was he to sell cheeses?

José wasn't a salesman, she discovered. His next and last civilian job was as teacher of calligraphy, algebra, geometry and Italian in the private school of Paulo Semedei, former Catholic priest whose book published in Paris had caused an uproar in papal circles. Semedei was ex-communicated, exiled. Garibaldi's students were of adolescent age. Twenty-odd years later Saturnino Ribes founded shipyards in Salto; José Antonio Tavarola became director of Uruguay's first national bank; Cayetano Alvarez founded Montevideo's leading daily, *El Siglo*.

Garibaldi was one of her teachers, too.

From the roof terrace she watched two successive naval battles between Uruguayan commander John Coe, US native, and legendary admiral of the Argentine fleet, William Brown, Welshman, formerly of US merchant navy and famous for his victories over the Brazilian fleet. Republican gunboat *Rivera* ran aground on a sandbank.

In behalf of the republic, port commander Captain Larobbla came to the house and begged Garibaldi to refloat the *Rivera*. As a result of his fighting in Rio Grande, Garibaldi was a household word in

Montevideo. She *was* the household.

In the dead of night, while she slept, José was in water again "warping" the *Rivera* off the sandbank. He lashed together two kedge anchors, fastened ropes to them and to the launch. Carrying the anchors, José and two sailors rowed the launch through the breakers. He dove in, holding the steel anchors, dug them in, surfaced and swam with ease back to the *Rivera*--like some sea-god. The *Rivera* moved one palm, another....

The *Rivera was* afloat.

Old salt Commodore Coe retired. Minister Francesco Vidal offered Garibaldi commander of Uruguay's naval squadron, rank of colonel in the army, officers' rations. His first mission was to go up the Parana River carrying supplies, troops to the allied province Corrientes.

Prominent Italians met in her house. Despicable, this Vidal, in no time he would be in Europe with treasury funds, riding around its first capitals in an expensive coach. His final stroke in getting rid of the navy was getting rid of Garibaldi. But a successful mission got rid of Vidal. It was 600 miles to Corrientes, Brown's fleet guarding the rivers. José would be able to land only on steppes, islands. The rivers weren't navigable this time of year for ships drawing more than 18 feet of water. The mission's flagship *Constitución* drew more than 18 feet.

Castellini spoke Italian to José:

"Peppino, tutti gli italiani qui vogliono che tu commandi. Anch'io lo voglio. Se tu accetti, prometto di attrezzare una nave per andare in Italia." "Peppino, all the Italians here want you to take command. I, too. If you accept, I promise to outfit a ship to take you to Italy."

José looked away. If they could reach Corrientes, they would command the Paraná, destroying enemy trade between the inner provinces and Paraguay and Buenos Aires.

She didn't seek to influence him.

Garibaldi accepted command of Uruguay's navy, rank of colonel, but with a soldier's, not an officer's, rations.

19. AN HONEST WOMAN

She married Garibaldi. Before he shipped out, she got married.

Marriage was her sacred duty. Either of them, especially José now, could be killed at any moment--a widow with a child, both nothing.

Still there was no news of Manuel Duarte.

A sailor she'd helped aboard the *Rio Pardo*--Giovanni, how many had she nursed?--came to Calle Porton for shelter and a job. Sailor Giovanni had news of Manuel Duarte--killed in a battle in the interior after Marshal Andréia gained control of Laguna.

Cuneo would know what to do. José spoke to him. Abbot Paul, Cuneo's good friend, would see to it the sailor's sworn statement was valid proof of Duarte's demise. As for José's side, he needed two witnesses to certify he was single and free to marry.

But then they couldn't find the sailor--he'd shipped out to Marseilles!

She spoke to Marta Moriani--friend, elder, dark-complexion, too, black hair streaked with silver. Cuneo was wrong. The sailor's sworn statement wouldn't have satisfied the Curia's requirements. She, Marta Moriani, was willing to tell the Curia she was the betrothed's mother and that her daughter was single and free to marry.

In the Apostolic palace's somber hall, Garibaldi appeared before the Notary, Padre Don Juan Pedro Gonzalez.

"I declare that being single and free, I wish to take Ana Maria de Jésus of Brazil to be my wedded wife, according to the ordinances of the Mother Church, Holy, Roman, Catholic, Apostolic."

Church authorities empowered the Notary to call upon Ana Maria de Jesus at her house.

She and Marta Moriani prepared, covering the table in the family room with a colorful cotton cloth and arranged wild flowers, three chairs around the table. The women rehearsed. Marta would say that she was Maria Antonia de Jesus, born in São Paulo, at an early age moved to the mountain district *Serra Rio do Rasto,* southern Brazil, where she met her husband, deceased now, Bentão da Silva, *tropeiro.* Spoke mountain dialect, couldn't write. Her daughter, Ana Maria, also couldn't write. As for who would sign, notaries always traveled with secretaries, their writing cases too heavy, so the secretary would sign.

Notary Don Juan Gonzalez arrived with a secretary carrying his writing case. Menotti beat the time with his wooden sticks against his stool. The Notary spoke, secretary transcribing:

"In my jurisdiction, I, the Notary, in virtue of the order verbally given to me by the proper authorities, went to the house of Ana Maria de Jesus, who, informed of the purpose of my visit, stated she was the single, legitimate daughter of Maria Antônia de Jésus, who was present, and Don Bentão da Silva and, in good faith, pledged her word..."

The next day, Good Friday in the church of San Francesco d' Assisi, Garibaldi handed the Curia a few coins, who in turn handed

Garibaldi a piece of paper--"Marriage License." Outside, José searched his pockets for money to buy gold wedding bands. He came up with his silver timepiece. He looked away...

His first ship *Costanza* had come to him as if in a magical dream, transformed to a luscious young woman, then his parents accompanied him to the pier. "Now the sea is your foster parent," his father, Padrone Domenico, had said, and his mother hugged him, crying, and gave him the silver timepiece.

José pawned the timepiece in exchange for two silver wedding bands.

March 26, 1842, a Saturday, Holy Saturday, church bells pealing all over the city, gold and white replacing purple hangings in San Francesco d' Assisi, she married Garibaldi. She'd made a wedding dress of various shades of green. Her wedding slippers didn't come off at the church door--good omen, rich girl. Did she feel deep in her heart that her church marriage to Garibaldi was bigamous?

Two months later, her husband aboard the flagship *Constitución* of 18 guns sailed out of the harbor, destination Corrientes, Argentina.

20. BATTLES WITH BROWN

She bore his first long absence with patience, cupboard half-empty.

Batteries on the island of Martín Garcia raked Garibaldi's three ships as they passed. Italian officer Pocaroba had his head blown off. Three miles beyond the island, the *Constitución* ran aground on a sandbank. In his effort to refloat her, Garibaldi transferred her cannon to the *Pareira* of two guns, encumbering her deck, so the gun couldn't be fired.

Meanwhile, Admiral Brown advanced with seven warships amid shouts of approval from the island's inhabitants. But just as Brown was about to fire broadside, his admiralship ran aground on sand. José wrote:

"One piece of luck, good or bad, rarely comes alone because then a dense fog engulfed the region and with a favoring wind we sailed toward the Parana."

Garibaldi's pilots were stubborn, apathetic. Pretending not to know the river, they refused further responsibility.

"I really didn't care about their responsibility, what I needed was a pilot and the quicker, the better. I quickly cleaned up all obstacles with my sword. Soon we had a pilot."

Needing smaller transport ships and helmsmen, in a nocturnal expedition they seized merchant vessels and landed to get food, mainly cattle, then for two miles sailed under a battery that seemed to hang over their heads. Finally, they reached Corrientes, joining its flotilla of two sloops and an armed cutter. They took in fresh provisions, troop reinforcements. Garibaldi addressed the men:

"This river is four palms' width less than necessary for the flagship's draught. Unable to continue, we must defend."

Water was deeper toward the left bank--here Garibaldi drew up his line of ships: first a small vessel newly mounted with four cannon; the *Pareira,* two-decker brig of 18 cannon, formed the center; the *Constitución,* corvette of 18 cannon, right wing. Battle order was vertical in the direction of the river, strongest side turned toward Brown. Though the water was shallow, the current was strong, so Garibaldi tied his ships together.

Admiral Brown's seven ships, able to receive reinforcements and provisions, advanced in a favorable wind.

The battle raged violently three days, with heavy losses on both sides. Garibaldi's ships were shot to pieces. Both sides sent men on land--they skirmished. Munitions exhausted, Garibaldi and crew broke up anchor chains, nails, any ironmongery. His flagship shattered, the *Pareira* sinking, Corrientes' flotilla deserting, Garibaldi had the wounded carried ashore. He laid four charges on each ship, scattering stores of gunpowder, torched his own ships and directed them toward Brown's.

Brown's ships exploded. The tremendous explosions stunned Brown into not pursuing.

"It was a terrifying and imposing sight to see the wreckage of the blown-up ships flying overland. At the spot of the explosion the river remained smooth as a mirror, but the debris was thrown far and wide onto both banks, even onto the right bank one mile away."

Gathering a few stragglers, Garibaldi returned to Montevideo.

It was December, he'd been away since June. She greeted him with blessed news he could see--Menotti wanted a sister.

Cuneo sent accounts of Garibaldi's battles with Brown to Giuseppe Mazzini in London. Mazzini published Cuneo's accounts in his paper *L'Apostolato Popolare*. Sailors smuggled copies from Genoa to Sicily inside barrels of pitch and pumice stone, bales of drapery, packages of sausages.

21. UNDER SIEGE

Her husband's return coincided with Montevideo being surrounded and cut off by land and sea. She had no horse, and Menotti's life was more in danger now than in the mountains of Rio Grande.

Crossing into Uruguay, taking Salto and Colonia in the north, then covering 300 miles in 51 days, General Oribe's 9,000 cavalry and 3,500 infantry pulling siege guns appeared on the hills surrounding Montevideo. The vast army camped in the hill-fort *Cerro* she'd noticed on first entering the city. Admiral Brown's squadron arrived to assist Oribe's land force. The supply ship *Oscar* ran onto the rocks, her crew abandoned ship.

She had her love back a few hours.

Hours after returning from Corrientes, José approached the wrecked *Oscar* with five small ships, boarded and removed all stores, guns and ammunition. Brown sent man-of-war *Palmar* and five small vessels against Garibaldi. He engaged them in a brisk gun battle, then retreated with captured stores.

Citizens, she and Menotti watched from high points in the city--windows, balconies, roof terraces. Every day for the next ten years, Brown's ships launched shells into the city, killing civilians.

José's grave concern was if Oribe launched a full-scale attack, the people's will to resist would find no match in the city's defenses. They had 2,000 soldiers, 140 cavalry, no navy to oppose Brown's fleet.

Why didn't Oribe launch a full-scale attack?

She understood cavalry wasn't experienced in street fighting. With such a show of force, perhaps Oribe expected the city to surrender. Or destroying Montevideo would turn international opinion against Rosas, who was supported by the papacy and England.

Minister Francesco Vidal fled to Europe with treasury funds, as she and her companions had foretold, at the very moment was riding around its first capitals in a fine coach, richly clad lady beside him.

New Minister-of-War, white-bearded Pacheco y Obes, who later on in Paris told Dumas about Garibaldi and her, Dumas writing a book "Montevideo or the New Troy," she not being a new Helen, merely citizen-soldier--Minister Pacheco called to arms all able-bodied citizens. "Build me a fleet," Pacheco told Garibaldi.

Of Montevideo's 42,000 citizens, more than half were immigrants, the majority political refugees of high morale. Pacheco abolished slavery, winning support of the Black population and powerful abolitionist movement in England. All slaves born in Uruguay since 1814 had already been freed; of the 6,000 newly freed, 4,000 joined the army.

Citizens rebuilt the city's old walls. Men, women, children threw up breastworks, dug trenches, melted down church bells and tore down balconies and gates from house fronts for the metal. Women from the different immigrant groups worked in the roads with shovels and pickaxes, took turns caring for the children, organized distribution of food, raised money.

She organized her ward, the harbor district.

Four months' pregnant, clasping Menotti close, she made her way around the city, bombs exploding. She and women of her ward went into houses and took down, gathered crucifixes and religious medals. They would replace the artifacts later on.

Posters plastered all over the city walls-- "Any foreigner taking up arms for the defense of the capital or aiding or abetting its citizens will be dealt with summarily as soon as the city falls into our hands."

"Summarily"--that is, Menotti hanged without a word.

She and Menotti passed long lines of women, children waiting for food rations. A recruiting office had a large sign outside, French Legion, volunteers waiting to go in and sign up. In return for fighting, French legionaries were granted 60 square miles and 25,000 head of cattle when the war was over. Three thousand Frenchmen signed up.

A Frenchman of some standing said to another Frenchman, overheard by an Italian: "An Italian Legion? Italians are good only for stabbing in the dark or from behind; care or money spent on them would be thrown away."

She wasn't Italian, her husband was.

A small legation of Italian men came to the house. She was in the other room, playing with Menotti. The Italians were going to challenge the French defamer of their nation to a duel, and wanted Garibaldi's personal support.

Garibaldi denied the Italians his support.

"But in your battle with Brown," the spokesman said, "dead

and wounded on your deck many, the rest worn out but unable to rest because of water rising in the hold--yet, still having some gunpowder and shot, you were bound, you said, to fight on, not for riches, but for honor."

"Honor! Don't make me laugh!" He was inclined to laugh when he thought of a soldier's honor. The honor of Bourbons, Spaniards, Austrians, French! The honor of the murderer who assaults a traveler on the high road! "The honor which makes us slaughter our fellow countrymen while a monster on the throne, a sceptered scoundrel [Pope Gregory XIV], enjoys the sight laughing in his sleeve amid the lurid revelry of Naples, Vienna, Madrid, Paris! And the people? Treated as fodder for such as these--" Piece of crockery, bowl of bean soup, crashed to the floor. Her husband raged on: "There's your honor and liberty and justice and laws! What's the advantage to the people, to those who toil and die of hunger? What's the advantage to those who throw away their lives, like you, you, you want to do? What's the advantage to the countless noble Italians driven into strange lands by the misfortunes of their country..." Mutru, Carniglia drowning; Rossetti, dead, kicked under his horse--all without stones to mark their bones. "What men! What services rendered! And how repaid!" José stormed into the family room, then out... "If one of us kills that Frenchman, what will it prove? That one man has dared to face a coward--" José must have looked away now--"We must grasp the opportunity to prove to the city that the Frenchman is a liar. Let's profit by the situation."

On April 13, 1843, a Thursday, ordinary day of bombs exploding far and near, macaroni-beans and getting Menotti safely through another day--at 8 a.m. his father opened a recruiting office with the sign outside, Italian Legion. Frugoni and Castellani helped, greeting volunteers who identified themselves by name and trade. Of 4,200 Italians in Montevideo, 400 of all types and from all classes signed on: merchants, students, doctors, artists, deserters from foreign warships, criminals wanted by the police. Unlike the French legionaries, Italian legionaries refused the land grant and cattle. Garibaldi was proud. She felt her husband's pride.

José was still colonel of the navy, his main concern breaking Brown's blockade of food, medicines and arms. Breaking the blockade could have an effect on France and England, who acted on the recognized rule of international law that a blockade was legal only if effectively enforced.

She and Menotti watched the spectacle from the roof terrace.

With his small, fast fleet, Garibaldi dashed, shooting, to the outer limits of Brown's blockade. The admiral's ships guarding the port entrance rushed up. Supply ships came in, smugglers of beef and arms. Garibaldi's ships retreated.

22. THE RED SHIRT

Without her dearest, the Italian Legion engaged in its first action, part of a large-scale sortie. First battalion under Danunzio captured enemy outposts--but the second and third battalions refused to advance, turning and running, claiming lack of ammunition.

She wasn't at the *Cerro* to bring up ammunition.

The populace and French legionaries jeered the Italians as they entered Montevideo. Their cowardice was talk of the town, the papers.

She sewed her husband's navy uniform--long, double-breasted, light-blue coat with gold buttons. José's everyday garb was baggy pants, shirt, poncho. When he wore his black beret, concealing his long golden hair, he passed unnoticed.

She passed unnoticed, too, no enemy man at hand to see her.

José liked to see his name in the papers--well, this time his name was in the papers big time. Colonel Garibaldi made poor choices of commanders, due to an overtrusting nature. The whole fiasco was caused by Garibaldi's laxity in disciplining troops.

Garibaldi: "If you train a man to face and fight the enemy, never to fire in the air or from a distance too great, nor turn his back on the field nor yield to a panic--it's as much as you can expect."

José wasn't a drill sergeant, she discovered.

One French scribe wrote that a French general would hang the cowards, there was no place in the army for a chief opposed to capital punishment, hanging, even flogging. Italian commander Garibaldi was simply *strano*: vegetarian in a land of beef, drank water with garlic in a land of wine, believed in women's rights of suffrage--"suffrage," that is, right to vote.

"I'm ready to die of shame and grief."

She felt her husband's shame, his grief.

José and she remembered Francesco Anzani. José had written down Mr. Anzani's new address on a piece of paper, in the pocket of the shirt Anzani had given to him--of all places Buenos Aires! José wrote to him by candlelight, inviting him to come to Montevideo.

Mr. Anzani came.

She grew to love Anzani in a deferential, formal way, marking him nevertheless for a glorious death, begun by the wound in his lung suffered in Portugal--"glorious," that is, in behalf of country, at the same time inspiring those still fighting.

The French Legion was put in uniform. So must the Italian.

Men of the city wore shirt, trouser, poncho. Men of the *pampa* wore baggy pants of undyed wool, like José, matching in color everyday pants woven by the Indians. The Italian legionaire's shirt should be striking in color and definitive--José had a passion for colors, Mr. Anzani was definitive in matters of discipline--in order to relieve the monotony of natural gray.

She and Mr. Anzani went to a French warehouse--clothes, bolts of fabric. She ran her hand over white shirts--too expensive. She was shown cloth, bolts of red cloth intended for the *saladeros*, slaughterhouses, of Buenos Aires, color red disguising the butchers' bloody work. Brown's blockade prevented shipment--the red cloth was a bargain.

Red was the color of the moment, cry of alert, President Bento Gonçalves had said. And standout color red froze a soldier thinking of turning, running.

Still, the Legion needed 500 shirts practically overnight.

"Buy the cloth, I'll guarantee the shirts."

The French proprietor threw in a lot of green cloth and a few thousand white buttons.

Italian artist Gallino designed a tunic, blouse, worn over the trousers and belted at the waist. Green cloth faced the collar, cuffs, center strips. Buttons were white.

She cut the first Red Shirt from Gallino's pattern, pinned it together, tried it on José in their kitchen.

An Original Red Shirt, Montevideo

Around this time Gallino painted a miniature portrait of her in her wedding dress refurbished with shawl collar of white silk.

Each woman of her ward found three other women who could cut and sew. Women cut, sewed the first 500 Red Shirts.

One hundred Italian legionaries in Red Shirts sailed across the bay toward the *Cerro*. Garibaldi unexpectedly came aboard.

The hill-fort was in Republican hands but was surrounded by Oribe's troops. The Italian Legion manned the front lines in a skirmish well into the black night. Lacking confidence in the Italian Legion's ability, the Montevidean commander didn't order an attack. Pacheco y Obes was in the field, Garibaldi appealed to him--enemy detachment entrenched in a house less than a mile away. Pacheco granted permission to attack the house.

Garibaldi exhorted the Red Shirts: "Today, June 10, we Italians are going to vindicate Italy's honor on foreign soil! You are all true heroes!"

Garibaldi in the lead, the Italian Legion stormed the house with bayonets, killed, put the enemy to flight, and returned to the *Cerro* with 43 prisoners.

A cheering crowd welcomed the Italian Legion into Montevideo.

She rode out to greet José. Together they rode into *Plaza de la Constitucion*.

The Italian and French Legions paraded side by side. Minister Pacheco awarded the Italian Legion their colors, black flag with a volcano in the center--volcano, symbol of Italy's sorrow, fire raging in her heart.

"Mr. Anzani, we may be satisfied, I think."

"No, we're not out of the wood yet."

"Don't exact too much from human frailty."

That night, by the light of candles, British Admiral H. Winningham Ingram wrote to his wife:

"Maria Ouseley, wife of ambassador Sir William Ouseley, was riding beside Colonel Garibaldi. Mrs. Ouseley is a citizen of the United States by birth, daughter of Cornelius Van Hess, one time governor of Vermont. Her tall, stately figure attracts attention wherever she goes. Today Anita Garibaldi suddenly rode up and reared her horse, frightening Mrs. Ouseley's horse and herself. Mrs. Garibaldi took her place beside the colonel and they rode in together. Anita Garibaldi is, from the habits of her country, a splendid horsewoman, and it is a sight to be remembered as she rides a curveting animal by the side of her husband."

23. JEALOUSY

Her husband was a celebrity now, Italian women and legionaries' wives stopping and thanking him. José was gracious and shy, nodding thanks. He received invitations from the best houses, perfumed paper intoxicating. He should go alone--she didn't have proper clothing for a woman eight months' pregnant. They stayed home.

Not one woman of her age, of the glory of Maria da Gloria, emerges from eight years in Montevideo.

Doña Bernadina, minister Pacheco's wife, chaired a committee of high society women in her lavish home, raising subscriptions for troop comforts. She went to one meeting but was ostracized. Her skin too dark, clothes too plain, too poor, the women's activities too tame?

There was Marta Moriani, non-combatant surrogate mother.

She raised money for an Italian Legion hospital, organizing a benefit at the *Teatro de Comercio*, few blocks from Calle Porton. She booked Montevideo's opera company in a performance of a Donizetti opera, popular with the Legion and her husband. He was always singing, humming some aria.

For the benefit performance, she wore her refurbished wedding dress, shawl collar of white lace. The house rose, cheered her and José's entrance. During intermission José was besieged by admirers, women asking to meet her, she sitting beside him.

At home she flew into a jealous rage.

Behind her, unclasping her dress, José tried to steady her by holding her arms. "These women with their exquisite hands and feet, small and well-formed as those of any high-born dame of Seville, are not attracted by the Legion or by one José Garibaldi--but by his hair."

"Is that why you wear it so long?"

Next morning on his way to port José stopped at the Legion's barracks. Captain Sacchi was the first to see him. "What on earth happened to your hair?"

"My wife claims I wear it long to attract the ladies, so I cut it."

She made Garibaldi cut his hair. No modern-day Delilah was she--never for a moment, one expedition, did she hold Garibaldi back. Quite the opposite--she gave him strength.

Nearing term, amid bombs exploding, she made her way holding Menotti through the streets to the Legion's hospital, volunteering, as in Laguna.

For her, poverty was a Republican virtue, as it was for Garibaldi. She was aware this early on of José's plan of one day returning to Italy with the Legion, one good reason he'd founded it, so they mustn't profit from theirs or the Legion's commitment to Uruguay's freedom.

Virtue brought with it multiple anxieties, Menotti eating at times crusts of stale bread, and there was dissension and treason in the Legion. And she found out through a wounded soldier's whisperings that the colonel, her husband, and Anzani, who'd gotten rid of commander Danunzio whom Garibaldi considered adequate, were targets of a hired assassin's knife.

José hadn't been home for weeks. She hadn't seen Mr. Anzani. She pleaded with Legion doctor Odichini to find, tell her husband about the assassination plot.

She was seized with labor pains in the dead of night, Menotti asleep. She dragged herself to the front door, fainted. Dr. Odichini found her wedged against the front door.

José was on his way.

He'd led an attack on Oribe's troops, a few legionaries entering civilian houses, including the Brazilian minister's, Edoardo Regis. Brazil and Uruguay were in negotiations, so Regis made a bargaining chip of Garibaldi's attack on his house, calling him a "notorious pirate," demanding his arrest and dismissal from the army. Brazil hadn't forgotten Rio Grande, neither had Garibaldi--he interpreted "notorious pirate" as a personal affront, went to the Brazilian ministry, walked up to Edoardo Regis and slapped his cheek. Staff officers standing around charged Garibaldi. He was carrying his walking stick with hidden sword, drew it. Staff officers backed away. José slapped Regis' other cheek. The minister refused the challenge. "Coward!" José called him, turned and left.

Uruguay had to do something--José was placed under house arrest on his flagship.

Dr. Odichini had sent a messenger to Pacheco, explaining the colonel's wife's condition. Regis was sent to Rio de Janeiro, Garibaldi home.

In the last days of June 1843, she gave birth to a baby girl whom she named Rosita, after the brave little republic in which she was born.

24. THE VIRTUE OF DARKNESS

"Anita, bring a light!"

"No light to bring!" She was on the roof terrace.

Usually José proposed meetings be held at the ministries, after dark. Once, English ambassador Sir William Ouseley asked him why-- Garibaldi was always sure of a welcome. He threw back his poncho, revealing a bare chest. For some reason, perhaps secrecy, Ouseley and French Admiral Lainé came to the house.

She was out of money for candles.

"Candles aren't part of the soldier's ration, gentlemen. We can talk just as well in the dark."

José, Ouseley and Lainé sat and spoke in the dark. Diplomatic efforts with dictator Manuel Rosas of Argentina failing, the governments of France and England ordered seizure of all Argentine vessels in the Rio de la Plata. Those governments wanted Garibaldi to command a joint French-English-Montevidean expedition--open communications with Brazil by destroying Rosas' fleet and occupy the island fortress Martín García and northern cities Colonia and Salto.

Garibaldi demanded 15 outfitted ships, 200 Italian legionaries, one national guard battalion, 100 cavalry fully armed and equipped, six artillery horses, two four-pounder cannon.

The next day Colonel Tajes came to the door, handed her 100 patacones to buy candles "in behalf of Minister Pacheco and the Uruguayan people".

She and José kept 12 patacones for candles, giving the rest to widow Danoel down the road.

Shortly before leaving on what's become known as Expedition Up the Uruguay River, considered by Garibaldi the finest in his career, including Sicily 15 years later when she wasn't present in body--the family went to Montevideo's annual carnival. There were marching bands, African dancers, jugglers, clowns in white face. With the settling in of the black night, citizens danced in the glow of Chinese lanterns. Rosita's big beautiful eyes fixed on a sad-looking man, not a clown, and kept smiling and making faces until a smile broke on the sad man's face. Precocious Rosita clapped.

25. A WORLD OF GRACIOUS THINGS

She spent the summer of sweltering heat safeguarding the children, waiting for the new baby and news of José. Rations grew irregular after his departure for the north on August 25, '45. Dr. Odichini and his wife found the cupboard half-empty, Menotti chewing on stale bread and Rosita with pneumonia.

Her father had a way of returning, doubling back so to speak, to scenes of previous adventures. Island fortress Martín Garcia surrendered without a fight. Garibaldi hoisted the Republican banner, took in oxen and horses, left behind a few men, continued up river. In the town of Gualeguay, Argentina, governor Leonardo Millan was captured.

She knew about Leonardo Millan, he'd tortured José, hanging him by the wrists from a roof beam two years before they met. She knew about Leonardo Millan from the chronic pain in José's wrists, which she comforted.

Captain Sacchi reported Millan's capture to Garibaldi.

"Set him free without bringing him into my presence. I don't wish to lay eyes on him."

In Colonia, charming town of white, 18th-century houses built in the Spanish colonial style, Garibaldi rendezvoused with the Anglo-French squadron.

Rosistas forced the inhabitants to burn their town. Colonia went up in flames.

The Italian Legion landed first, pressed the enemy. The Allies occupied the devastated city, appropriating property scattered in the streets, mainly mattresses. Amid the rubble and burnt-out places, José tried to prevent rape and looting.

He was most enthusiastic after his first meeting with the *matrero,* gaucho of the mountain ranges. He met Vivorigna and his companion, Miranda. Most impressive was Juan de la Cruz Ledesma with his black headdress, eagle eyes, noble bearing and fine character. Juan de la Cruz and Scotsman Joseph Mundell, brought to this country at an early age, brave, with refined manners, would remain unforgettable. These *matreros* brought in other *matreros,* forming a cavalry of 100.

The *matrero,* Garibaldi wrote, was truly an independent man, in that part of South America often ruled over an extensive stretch of land. He did not levy taxes and duties, but demanded and received from the inhabitants what he needed for his wandering life. A good horse, carbine, pistol, sword and knife were inseparable companions. He used his knife with a strange ability in wounding and slitting the enemy's throat. He swam rivers holding his knife in his teeth, often wounded the enemy from the stream. He hit the tired horses with his *bolas,* jumped aground, slit the enemy's throat, jumped back on his horse to catch up with another.

"When the *matrero* enters his house, he finds there one who truly loves him and shares his hardships and dangers with endurance and strength of soul which equals his. Woman, according to me the most perfect creature, seems by nature more chivalrous and more ready for adventure than man, and it can only be ascribed to the slavish upbringing to which she is condemned in that country if examples of heroism are to be found so rarely."

She might have smiled.

Anzani directed the vanguard with a few small vessels and captured merchant vessels--in this way they reached the Jaquary River, the Jaquary flowing into the Uruguay and Rio Negro Rivers.

It was in the Rio Negro she and José had lost 400 head, Menotti barely a year old riding in a small, pony-driven cart, protected from bumps by ponchos and blankets wrapped around him.

The Rio Negro formed several islands covered with forest and pasture, was practically inhabitable because of frequent flooding--here the troops rested, and rested the horses. On the other side of the island rose the promontory *Rincon de las Galinas,* connected to the mainland by an isthmus. This promontory was the *matreros'* favorite place. The Rosistas tried to send inhabitants into the interior to sever connection with the Republicans. Many inhabitants joined, were received cordially. José was creating safe havens in enemy territory, restoring property, releasing political prisoners. The Uruguay River's largest island became a small colony of refugee families--from Montevideo, too. José wrote to Cuneo, Cuneo reported to her. José's PS's read like this:

"Send me, I beseech you, 250 pairs of shoes, 50 pairs of boots." "Send me 250 caps, 200 *ponci,* jackets for the sailors."

For several days Juan de la Cruz didn't return from the *Rincon de las Galinas*. Garibaldi worried, from other *matreros* learned that Juan and his cavalry had fought several irregular bands; yielding to superior forces, Juan had let his forces scatter. Garibaldi sent Juan's companion Saldana to find him.

Juan de la Cruz in black headdress had fled into the forest's innermost thicket, abandoning his horse found a canoe and set out for a hiding place. Saldana approached an island completely under water, save one tree. Juan's canoe was tied to this tree, Juan himself hiding in it.

From that day on, all the *matreros* of the surrounding districts joined the expedition, increasing the cavalry to 500.

Horses, cloth were needed.

From a height overlooking the Uruguay's left bank, Garibaldi saw a spacious farmhouse with roof terrace, *ranchos* all around, barracks, herds of tame oxen, wild cattle, herd of 40,000 sheep spread far over the field. In quiet times the owner had many slaves. *Hervidero*, formerly a splendid settlement, was now empty, deserted, enlivened only by raging, seething whirlpools, making the reef-studded river like a cauldron of boiling water. Anzani took possession of the settlement.

From scouts sent out by Juan de la Cruz, Garibaldi learned that the famous *matrero* Joseph Mundell was at the Arroyo Malo, 30 miles below the waterfall, or *Salto*. Mundell's influence had gathered several thousand, and he wanted to join the expedition. Garibaldi went to see him.

On Garibaldi's first night's absence, enemy generals Garzon and Lavelleja attacked *Hervidero,* Garzon with 2,000 holding the river's right bank, posting two burning ships to prevent Republican sailors from assembling land forces, Lavelleja attacking with cavalry.

Mr. Anzani instructed his men: "Don't fire until they're so close our shots burn their coats."

Lavelleja's cavalry approached...

Anzani's men waited, waited, then--a murderous fire! Smoke covered the field of dead, wounded.

Garibaldi arranged with Joseph Mundell to come to Salto.

José and his staff were eating. A courier brought the mail. She'd given birth to a girl--Teresita! Few weeks later the courier delivered another letter, from Minister Pacheco: "Your daughter Rosita is dead. This you ought to know at any rate."

"She was the most beautiful, sweetest of little girls. *Era un mondo di cose gentili.* A world of gracious things was that child.

"Pacheco isn't a father, never has been, never could be. The way the news was communicated was so brutal, hurt me so grievously that from that moment his memory was repugnant to me."

Anzani suggested she come to Salto with the children. The rivers were clear. He would send two men. One was Aguyar. Son of slaves born on the *estancia* of General Aguyar, Andrea Aguyar was a giant of a black man, professional horsebreaker, body of a perfect athlete. Rosita had been his pet.

26. THE GLORY OF SALTO

She'd buried Rosita in a small white casket, planted flowers and lit candles. Captain Lavagna helped her.

Andrea Aguiar appeared at her side, never to leave her in time of danger, marking him for a glorious death. Now she, Menotti, Teresita and Andrea Aguiar traveled 500 miles along Uruguay's great rivers Rosita didn't see.

The gentle women of Salto decorated the colonel's headquarters with flowers of the living, prepared for the children.

Hers and Rosita's words are heard:

"At the end she told me not to grieve. 'We'll meet soon, *mamãe*, meet to part no more.' Is there an afterlife, José?"

"Yes, we shall see our Rosita again. This little bit of *miseria* is but an episode of immortality, part of an infinite flame animating the universe."

Joseph Mundell arrived with 100 other *matreros*. They needed cloth, horses.

From José's high observation point overlooking the Uruguay River, she watched with him all day and the next. Around noon horses came to the opposite bank to feed, drink. Nearby, sentinels of reconnaissance cavalry rested in the shade of distended ponchos. The horses returned to the bank in the evening.

José wasn't going for the horses. He'd lined up boats at the shore. She and José watched.

Twenty *matreros*, knives in teeth, waited. At the signal they rushed to the mile-wide river, threw themselves in. One company of legionaries set off in the boats. The *matreros* swam holding on to their horses' manes and tails, baggage and guns in a leather pocket tied to the harness. Reaching the opposite bank, the *matreros* emerged from underwater on their horses, then quiet as mice mingled their horses with horses already there, shielded by the sun crept up on the sentinels.

The sentinels awoke to whistling of bullets and seeing *matreros* charging, retreat cut off by the legionaries mounted now and positioned on the hills. The sentinels were tied up, brought back on the boats. The *matreros* rounded up horses and drove them into the river and across.

At noon, February 8, 1846, she watched her husband ride into his glory, followed by 100 cavalry under Colonel Baez and 186 Red Shirts.

Reorganized Uruguayan army under new commander-in-chief General Medina advanced toward Salto to lift the siege, refugees with him. José's mission was to escort the general into enemy-controlled territory.

José marched out slowly, black silk scarf around his face, then north along the riverbank. The landscape was flat, the soil red. About one mile inland, near the San Antonio River, a hill rose 30 feet, angle so steep the top of a man's head walking up couldn't be seen on the other side until three steps from the summit. The area was open, dotted by clumps of orange trees. José reached the base of the hill. From two lengths shooting distance, 900 enemy cavalry and 300 infantry with banners unfurled poured over the top.

Colonel Baez: "Let's retreat." They were outnumbered six to one.

"No time." Garibaldi charged into the 186 legionaries. "The enemy are numerous, we are few! The more glorious will be the fight!"

He found a ruin--bombed-out building open on the west, wall on the east facing the enemy. Several posts driven into the ground remained, a legionary posted behind. Remaining legionaries formed three small divisions behind the ruin. Colonel Baez and his cavalry stood on the infantry's right, carabineers dismounted, lancers remaining on horseback.

Colonel Baez retreated after his first sharp encounter with Colonel Gomez' cavalry.

Three hundred enemy cavalry charged the ruin in a long straight line instead of column, surprising Garibaldi.

Hold fire until the enemy was within 30 yards. 100 yards, 50, 30--legionaries opened fire! 100 infantry went down.

Their bugle boy, 15-year-old Rufus, sounded the broken beat of attack. Red Shirts charged out in a compact mass with mad courage, beat back enemy infantry.

Gomez' cavalry returned from chasing Colonel Baez and with infantry attacked repeatedly throughout the scorching afternoon and into the night, coming close enough for hand-to-hand combat. Enemy cavalryman approached the ruin, torches in hands. His lobs went awry. Garibaldi prevented him from being shot.

Casualties mounted. Every Republican officer was killed or wounded, Captain Sacchi shot in the leg. The bugle boy was run through. Dying, the boy lunged with his knife and teeth. The bugle boy's and cavalryman's corpses locked together, the boy's full of wounds, the cavalryman's with teethmarks.

The Battle of San Antonio lasted nine hours. Their worst hardship was thirst under a burning sun. The Republicans retreated at nine o'clock.

The Uruguay River's trees afforded protection. They had a mile to go to reach the river. They had 33 killed, 35 wounded. The wounded lay across horses, those who could stand limped along, supported by two soldiers. José carried Sacchi. They marched along in close column. When the enemy came too close--"Right face, fire!" And sharpshooters kept up a steady fire. Their ranks thinned unexpectedly, the enemy stopped pursuing. In this way the Republicans advanced along the river, retreat taking three hours.

Midnight, she and Anzani waited at Salto's gate. Citizens rushed up to give all possible aid.

Next morning a burial corps, including French medical officer Desrosseaux who'd fought as a common soldier, dragged four carts to the battlefield covered with corpses and wounded from both sides. They were carried on the carts back to Salto.

The battle was memorable the first days after it--victims were given a ceremonial burial. On a height overlooking Salto, soldiers dug a mass grave and shoveled earth until a burial mound arose. A cross was planted with the inscription: *Legione Italiana, Marinai Cavalleria Orientale, 8 Febbrajo 1846.*

27. FAME

Press clip: "Garibaldi's 300 defeat Gomez's 1,200!"

Odes and rhapsodies were published in Italian and Spanish, recited, played at *Téatro do Commercio*. Marradi's *Rapsodia Garibaldina*:

> Oh verdi, interminabili, deserte
> distese della Pampa! oh pascolanti
> saure, del fren della sua mano esperte!

(O, endless green deserts
stretching across the pampas! O, grazing sorrels,
> reined in by her expert hand.

> Ivi ella crebe con l'alte erbe ondanti,
> ivi Ei le apparve, biondo come il sole,
> e la guarda con gli occhi scintillanti...

(There she grew up among the tall and waving grasses.
> here he appeared to her, blond like the sun,
> and he looked at her with sparkling eyes...)

Cuneo's newspaper *Il Legionario Italiano* commemorated the victory of San Antonio with a special issue, copies mailed to Mazzini in London. *The London Times* refused to publish, so Mazzini published Cuneo's accounts in his own paper, thousands of copies distributed underground throughout Italy. At the Scientific Congress in Genoa, cheers greeted mention of the name "Garibaldi". In Florence a subscription of 100 lire was opened for purchase of a Sword of Honor to be made by the renowned silversmiths of *Ponte Vecchio*. Signatures covered hundreds of parchment sheets. "Even the stones would sign, if they could," Mazzini wrote to his mother.

Garibaldi was made general. He refused promotion in a letter to Pacheco y Obes:

"As chief of the Italian Legion, whatever I have received as a reward I give to the mutilated men and families of the dead of the said Legion. Not only the rewards but also the honors would weigh on my soul, as they have been bought with Italian blood. The Legion found me as colonel and accepted me as such to be its head, and as such I shall leave the Legion when we have fulfilled our vows to the Uruguayan people."

José's rise to international fame was accompanied by a mood even she couldn't fathom. He was ponderous, silent for long periods. At times it appeared he wanted to settle in Salto, himself temporary dictator. He liked that the women of Salto, gentle *Saltegne,* were very friendly to the men. He summoned Cuneo and legionaries in Montevideo to Salto.

In contact with Mazzini and whirlwind events in Italy, Cuneo urged José to return to Montevideo.

José was disgusted, disillusioned. Fructuoso Rivera had seized power in a coup, splitting the army. Without Anzani, discipline failed in the Legion. Rivera issued a proclamation of praise for the Italian

Legion, then secretly contacted General Medina, ordering him to prevent the Legion from declaring for Pacheco and to hold Salto in his, Rivera's, behalf. Medina and Colonel Baez inflicted unmerited insults on the Legion, offered bribes to the cavalry.

José was clearing out as well as gathering. He cleared out Medina, writing to Salto's chief of police, Colonel Jaurequi:

I send herewith the order to Señor Brigadier-General Don Anacleto Medina to transfer himself on board the French warship *Eclair*, and I hold you responsible for the prompt execution of the order.

General Medina was awakened, escorted in his slippers to the *Eclair*. She set sail for Montevideo.

Mr. Anzani was down with consumption, the lung shot through in Spain. He wanted to die on Italian soil. And she was pregnant. It was August, baby would come at the end of February. José suggested she and the children go to Nice, stay with his mother--they would be safe there. He would follow with the Legion. She agreed, on the condition his plans to follow were definite.

José wrote to Cuneo: "I have finally decided to send my family to Nice, and as we are utterly impecunious, I shall be much obliged to you if you will help them obtain passage."

She returned to Montevideo, the family all together for the first time aboard a flagship, along the great rivers of Uruguay.

28. PASSAGE TO ITALY

She was uncertain about José's next big move. And the enemy still wasn't close at hand crossing a river with cattle and horses, in her face with a knife. The enemy was hidden now, corrupt, in shadows larger than giant fig trees. José needed time to work through.

Whirl of celebrations greeted them in Montevideo. The Basque Legion played the Italian Legion ashore and there was a victory parade, at night fireworks illuminated the capital.

She stayed aboard. She knew where Rosita lay, close by again. The next afternoon she ushered José to his daughter's grave.

As always she had little time to settle in.

Rising insubordination in the army after Rivera's coup moved all factions into pressing her husband to take command of the garrison--that is, become military governor of Montevideo. As always José waited. New baby grew in her stomach.

The Black regiment had mutinied over four months' back pay, had taken over the hill-fort *Cerro*. Pacheco's brother-in-law, Colonel Estivão, had tried to intercede and was killed--after that, no military chief would contend with the Black regiment.

José accepted the position military governor. The Black regiment got their back pay.

This baby wouldn't be born in Italy, perhaps the next one.

Could it be José was going away again merely to humiliate

Dictator Manuel Rosas, mop-up operation, raiding Argentine shipping along the *Rio de la Plata,* as far up the Parana as necessary, in the Argentine warship *Maipu?* Britain and France had compelled Admiral Brown and English-born officers to retire from the Argentine navy, then the foreign countries blockaded Buenos Aires. José came home on November 4 (1846), sailing the *Maipu* into the harbor, followed by 18 captured Argentine vessels.

A United States paper, *Daily Union* of Washington D.C., upbraided the English for sending "the Italian pirate Garibaldi" against Argentine shipping--in an Argentine ship!

Dictator Rosas wrote a personal letter to General Oribe:

"You should try to win the gringo Garibaldi, who is the inspiration of the savage Unitarians besieged in Montevideo, without stinting the amount. You should give him all the money he asks for, as the savages have not got any to give him, not even for candles."

Garibaldi was offered the bribe in front of Montevideo's new military governor, in his office--command of Argentina's navy, substantial salary, outright bonus $30,000 cash. Garibaldi got up and left without saying a word.

Oribe replied to Rosas: "I've used all possible means but he can't be won. He's a stubborn savage."

Death approached Porton Street. Argentine novelist Florencio Varela, according to Rosas representing middle-class Unitarian intelligentsia, lived at 90 *Calle de Misiones,* two hundred yards down the street. Hired assassins stabbed Varela in the back in front of his house. A fire broke out in the night in the tobacconist's shop next door. She urged on the fire brigade, fire extinguished. It wasn't accidental, she believed.

Nor was baby Ricciotti accidental, born fine and healthy on February 24 ('48), named for the Calabrian patriot Nicola Ricciotti, who three years earlier, facing his firing squad, sang the chorus of Mercandante's *Donna Caritea:* "He who dies for his country has lived long enough."

The Sword of Honor made through Italian subscription and fashioned by silversmiths of the *Ponte Vecchio,* gilt with silver and gold, hand-chased figures representing battle scenes, arrived in Montevideo. Small legation of Italian men presented the Sword to Garibaldi and the Legion in the main square, crowd cheering. She hung the spectacular, unwieldy Sword on the wall of her spare family room. They were poor as ever.

Teresita--called "Tita" by her father--fell down and cut her forehead. Her father promised to buy her a toy after his meeting, took three pesos from her money box. Somebody robbed the money box!

In June, England changed governments and sent Lord Howden and Count Welewski, Napoleon I's illegitimate son with Polish Countess Maria Wilenski, to negotiate a peace. Rosas was to recognize Uruguay's independence, withdraw troops. Foreign legions in Montevideo were to be disbanded, a caretaker government to arrange free elections for a new assembly that would elect a new president.

As in Rio Grande, the "peace" was unacceptable.

Garibaldi wrote about the negotiations: "The English-French intervention was supervised by disloyal, intriguing men."

Finally, the reason for José's delaying was at hand--what would Italian legionaries have once the war was over? They had refused President Rivera's gift of land and cattle, the new government would confiscate Uruguay's land. She couldn't go on and become precursor of the revolution in Italy, until Italian legionaries in Montevideo were settled.

Lord Howden tried to persuade Garibaldi to dissolve the Italian Legion, accept the peace terms. He refused--he had the support of the French and Italian Legions to continue the fight for Uruguay's freedom. Then Colonel Venancio Flores, Uruguayan, told Garibaldi unless he resigned as commander-in-chief there would be mutiny in Montevideo's army, native-born Uruguayans refusing to serve under him. Garibaldi resigned for the public good.

Sardinian ship *Carolina* arrived with a supply of revolutionary newspapers. Pius IX, succeeding Gregory XIV, had proclaimed amnesty to all political prisoners, relaxed censorship, abolished discriminatory laws against Jews, discontinued prosecution of heretics, laymen as well as priests could serve in high branches of government and the judiciary! Demonstrations, risings all over Italy: "*Viva Pio Nono e la liberta!*"

She knew Italy through Edoardo Mutru, Luigi Carniglia, Luigi

Rossetti, Cuneo. José's Rome was a true, deep link with Italy. His first and last trip to the Eternal City had been with his father, 1825, Peppino was 18. It was also Holy Year, sanctified by Gregory XIV with two waves of executions in Ravenna--men suspected of liberal sympathies hung after farcical trials, their bodies left to decompose on public gibbets; prisons throughout the papal states filled with similar suspects who, without charge or trial, were chained to walls and left to rot in their own excreta. José wrote passionately:

"Still, the Rome I beheld with my youthful imagination was the Rome of the future--the Rome that, shipwrecked, dying, banished to the furthest depths of the American forest, I have never despaired of: regenerating idea of a great nation, dominant thought and inspiration of my entire life. I worship her with all the fervor of a lover, not only the haughty bulwarks of her secular greatness, but the merest fragment of her ruins. This love I hid away as a secret treasure in the depths of my heart. It's a passion which, far from diminishing, has strengthened with distance and time. For me, Rome is Italy, and I see no Italy save in the union of its mutilated parts."

José and Mr. Anzani wrote a letter to Monsignor Bedini, papal nuncio in Montevideo:

"If these hands, which are used to fighting, would be acceptable to His Holiness, it is unnecessary to say we dedicate them most willingly to the service of him who has done so much for our country. We would indeed be very happy if we could co-operate in

Pius IX's work of redemption...and we do not think we would pay too high a price if it costs us our blood. We pray that His Holiness may be granted many years for the happiness of Christianity and of Italy."

Bedini sent the letter on to Rome, wrote to Garibaldi and Anzani "the devotion and generosity in your letter towards our supreme Pontiff is worthy of Italian hearts." Within two years, Pius IX would be their determined enemy, Monsignor Bedini endorsing their executions.

At night, in the dark of her house, José sent Giacomo Medici to Italy--make arrangements with Mazzini for a landing on Tuscany's coast.

She prepared to go to Italy with the children, wives and, if they had them, children of about 60 Italian legionaries. She would be meeting her mother-in-law the first time. José had been writing to his mother for years that he was married, not a word about poverty. She accepted clothing for the children from Dr. Odichini and his wife. As the time of embarkation approached, she broke down and begged José to let her go with him and the Legion.

He would probably be landing on Tuscany's coast and starting a revolution. And, again, he needed her to go ahead, among other things to acquire letters they would need.

She packed, carefully wrapping remnants of white, green and red cloth.

"What are you going to do with those rags?"

"Make a flag, carry it out when I see your ship."

Early next morning she visited Rosita with roses, knelt, ran her hand over stone, picked a bud, kissed it and pressed it in the colorful handkerchief in which she'd carried Menotti through the mountains of Rio Grande.

PART III: Italy (1848-49)

29. A WOMAN OF LEISURE

Sketch of Anita, artist unknown

Her ship passed the Azores, land of her ancestors. Of all the ships, magical or not, of Garibaldi's long, natural life, the one she and the children took to Italy--sailing vessel, eight weeks crossing the Atlantic in a winter storm--doesn't have a name. And not a word about the children--what kind of things did they do? Menotti beat his wooden sticks, it's been written. Did Teresita read, improving on her mother? She must have breastfed Ricciotti, who slept a lot, as babies do on ships in sea storms. She sewed together fragments of green, white, red cloth. She made an Italian flag at sea.

The Italian coastline came into view--Genoa's majestic palaces set on the ancient republic's steep slopes.

News of her coming had reached the Italian people. Small crafts came out, arms waving tricolors, patriots shouting: "*Viva Garibaldi! Viva Italia!*"

In their hearts she was the link to Garibaldi.

She carried Ricciotti. Their first touch with Italy, Menotti and Tita got lost, Menotti wandering off, as his father would, Tita's fingers slipping from her mother's skirt. Her friend waiting for them, Paolo

Antonini, returned the children, smiling. Antonini had returned from Montevideo to his home in Genoa, on a steep slope center of town. She handed the good friend a letter:

"I need not recommend my family to your care, as I know your heart only too well. I merely ask you to see them safely to my mother's house in Nice. My friends and I are resolved to return to Italy to offer our services either to the pope or to the grand duke of Tuscany."

A cheering crowd of three thousand gathered below the first-floor window. One man climbing on shoulders handed her a silk tricolor.

"For Garibaldi, Signora, to plant on the soil of Lombardy."

First time in her short, glorious life she was a lady of leisure--children cared for, cook preparing meals, coach and two waiting. She received a standing ovation at famous *Carlo Felice* opera house. How José, called Peppino in his country, was loved and longed for. He was aboard every ship hailing from Montevideo.

At the first opportunity she wrote a letter, written and mailed in Genoa, land of her husband's ancestors, to her host's brother, Stefano, in Montevideo. Her role as precursor to revolution began by delivering the news to José and their companions.

"Italian affairs go well. In Naples, Tuscany and Piedmont the constitution has been promulgated, and Rome is soon to have one. The national guard is everywhere established, and is of great benefit to these provinces. The Jesuits and all their agents have been expelled from Genoa and the entire province, and nothing is talked of save the union of Italy by means of political and custom-house leagues, and the liberation of Lombardy from the foreign yoke. I have received a thousand delicate attentions for your brothers Antonini. Yesterday I went to the opera; tonight I am going to the theatre, and have visited all the city and suburbs; and tomorrow I go by steamer to Nice. Be so kind, if my husband has not sailed already, as to hasten his departure, and tell him the latest events in Italy."

Most likely she passed through Piazza Sarzana, major landmark of her husband's past, where he'd begun his miraculous escape 15 years ago, good woman Natalina Pozzo hiding him in her fruit shop--"Women are angels in situations of this kind"--giving him peasant's clothes, putting fruit and cheese in his hat.

As requested, non-combatant, wealthy good friend Paolo Antonini accompanied her and the children to Peppino's mother in Nice. Their boat skirted the arching coastline José had shown her on charts in their kitchen. Lush gardens shining in the Riviera sun sprawled between villages and down to the curving coastline, Alpine foothills beyond. The children saw the water blue, like the sky, unlike the brown water like mud of the *Rio de la Plata*. Why was the *Rio de la Plata* called "Silver" when its water was brown? In the time of their ancestors the *Rio de la Plata* was named for a dream, the dream that one day treasures of the North--gold, silver, diamonds--would float downriver. Dreams and treasures could be brown, too.

Peppino hadn't been home in 14 years, hadn't seen his mother and father Padrone Domenico's resting place in all that time. Now she picked Donna Rosa out of the crowd waiting at the pier, recognizing the remarkable resemblance mother-son: high, almost square, forehead; slanted, piercing eyes; aquiline nose with broad root. Donna Rosa was in her mid-sixties, erect, head high, white kerchief around her head, like a turban.

She had trouble with her mother-in-law. Rosa Nicoletta Raimondi, daughter of fisherfolk and wife of a merchant captain, saw that her son's bigamous wife, mother of his children, was dark-complexioned and, since she wasn't really his wife, they couldn't sleep together under her roof.

The old woman lead the way to the *Quai Lunel*, just across from the waterfront. Nice--that is, *Nizza*, as the town had been settled by Italians from the mainland--was hot, faded pink. The house was the same faded pink and the way José had described it--bakery shop at street level, five dormers decorating the center of the roofline, wooded hills beyond; upstairs two floors of airy rooms, 13 tall windows edged in white on each floor, crucifixes and rosaries everywhere.

In the name of King Charles Albert, who'd decreed Peppino's death penalty 14 years ago, the city superintendent offered Menotti Garibaldi a free place in the royal college of Racconigi, near Turin. She was only the wife of Garibaldi and couldn't make such an important decision without first consulting with her husband.

Without her consent, Donna Rosa enrolled Menotti in a

Catholic school. The boy was easy to go and get, being the only dark-complexioned child in school.

Under cover of deep night, she met with a forger. One address José had given to her was the forger's.

On March 10 ('48), she received a letter from José. A very practical man, he wouldn't send a letter unless he knew the recipient could read it.

"Some unpleasant incidents are delaying our departure. Anzani has had a violent relapse and we feared Sacchi might lose his leg. Take care of my poor old mother for my sake and also dispel all the foolish notions old age may have suggested to her. My mother has always been so kind. When you walk through the places that witnessed my childhood, remember the companion of your ideals who so greatly loves you and greet them in my name. Embrace for me Menotti, Tita, Ricciotti, and my dear mother."

"When you walk through the places that witnessed my childhood...greet them in my name..."

"Peppino," she greeted his first home on the other side of the harbor, where Italians lived in a cluster. The house was heavily lidded, in an alley without name or number--locals called the alley *choù di buoù*, tail of the ox. "Dark, dingy, filthy and squalid," Europe's aristocrats described the alleys of Nizza'a ancient quarter. "Flies abound and windows are opaque with dirt and flyspecks. The Italians have to wash their windows every day or cover them with silk."

"Peppino," she greeted the seashore just across the alley where he'd played with his first toys: sea urchins, algae, crabs, spiders. Vessels gay with bunting sailed silently in and out of the harbor. The lighthouse cast its beam across the night sky. Masts shone silver, white in the moonlight. Seabirds fished and cried, and Peppino had heard other songs, those of the sailors and wounded veterans of the Napoleonic Wars turned beggars, composers of sea-songs:

I'm blind and I'm cripple yet cheerful would I sing

Were my disasters triple, 'cause why? Twas for my king.

"Peppino," she greeted the ancient quarter where Carnival had been. Huge floats decorated with cut flowers had paraded through the narrow streets. There'd been clowns with high-tufted collars, band with a big drum. Aristocrats marched in costumes and masks for the ball afterwards. The main event was the Battle of the Flowers: courtesans tossing bouquets of flowers at one another from horse-drawn carriages, the crowd tossing confetti and pistachios.

"Peppino," she greeted the wooded hills behind his hometown, where he'd listened to the nightingales' melodious chaplets and lain in the fields and listened to the flowers seek to breathe.

Young Garibaldi, sculpture by Fontana

"Peppino," she greeted the Paillon River which meandered through a gravel bed, filling and raging during a storm. At the age of eight, on his way home from a hunting expedition in the Var District just across the French frontier, Peppino had sat at the edge of the raging Paillon. Women washed clothes, steeped hemp. One woman slipped, fell in. Though short for his age, and encumbered by his game pouch, Peppino plunged in. One knee braced on the drowning woman's shoulders, he'd pulled--pulled up dead weight, sodden rags, arms and neck straining, head up, mouth open in a cry.

30. SPERANZA, OR HOPE

She pulled Garibaldi to his homeland.

He was beside himself with impatience, vexations.

"We shall arrive too late. We shall arrive when all is over. I must see my family."

Montevideo's government, especially its merchants, begged Colonel Garibaldi to stay, offering a house, plenty of food and land for Italian legionaries. Montevideo allowed Garibaldi to purchase a ship, *Speranza,* meaning Hope, with money raised by the Italians there, and Antonini followed through on his promise if not with a ship, then with provisions and arms. The majority of legionaries decided not to go, the expedition too hazardous.

On the eve of departure, José and Captain Lavagna who'd helped her bury Rosita stole into the cemetery and exhumed Rosita's small, white coffin, enclosed it in a metal case and carried it aboard the *Speranza.*

Dawn of April 15, 1848, with a favoring breeze though the weather threatened, the *Speranza* sailed out of the *Rio de la Plata's* great mouth, carrying 68 legionaries, the dog Guerello wounded at San Antonio, two cannon, 800 muskets and a good stock of gunpowder.

Citizens waved from windows, balconies, roof-terraces.

Toward evening the *Speranza* was between the Maldonado coast and *Isola di Lobos.* Next morning only peaks of *Sierra de las Animas* were distinguished, then the mountains disappeared--in view now was the vast level of the Atlantic.

"Our hearts throbbed with lofty hopes and enthusiasm."

During hours not spent in navigation, Andrea Aguyar led gymnastics on deck and the better educated taught the unlettered men. Colleli composed a rousing anthem, their evening prayer. Some brandy caught fire. Garibaldi and Mr. Anzani put out the fire. "Even brave men become frightened when faced with unaccustomed dangers."

Provisions suitable for Mr. Anzani exhausted, the *Speranza* anchored off Santa Pola, Spain. Captain Gazzola went ashore. He returned on the double with Anzani's provisions and incredible news: Naples, Sicily, Venice had revolted! Five days of streetfighting in Milan by an unarmed populace defeated the Austrian army's Croat regiment! Louis Phillipe and Chancellor Metternich were overthrown! All Italy was sending contingents north to the Holy War!

The men embraced, wept for joy. Anzani sprung to his feet, Sacchi insisted on being carried up. "Make all sail!"--destination Nice.

Morning of June 23, after a voyage of 68 days, the *Speranza* anchored in Nice.

31. THE LAGGO MAGGIORE CAMPAIGN

She rowed out to the *Speranza,* the tricolor she'd made on the Atlantic fastened and waving from an oarlock. She reunited joyfully with her husband, friends.

Practically all of Nice turned out and gave Garibaldi and the Legion a thunderous welcome ashore.

Peppino reunited joyfully with his children, mother. He handed the children the dog Guerello. That day the family set Rosita to rest beside paternal grandfather Domenico Antonio Garibaldi (1786-1841), merchant captain who in his day could find any Mediterranean port blindfolded. She told Peppino they couldn't sleep under the same roof. Donna Rosa had forbidden it. Peppino solved the problem by sleeping with his wife under his old sailor friend Deidery's roof.

Then she briefed Peppino. The news he'd heard off Santa Pola was true but not the whole of it. Most of Italy had constitutional governments but neither King Ferdinand of Naples nor Leopold of Tuscany nor Pius IX had the least intention of abdicating in favor of unity. In fact, these monarchs thwarted departure of students and workmen to the battlefields up north, where, in April, King Charles Albert of Piedmont with an army of 96,000 men had declared war against Austria. Liberals and reactionaries knew their fate was linked to Milan's. Driven out by Milan's unarmed citizenry, Austrian Marshal Radetsky fell back on the Quadrilateral--the fortresses of Verona, Mantua, Peschitia and Legnago. The Austrian empire existed there, in the fortresses. The entire north was divided between the monarchical party wanting all liberated provinces to vote for fusion with Piedmont, and the Republicans--that is, Mazzini and followers--wanting a federation of democratic states, exactly what Bento Gonçalves da Silva had wanted for the land of Brazil.

Peppino hadn't arrived too late, all wasn't over. In fact, the Revolution in Italy was just beginning.

Maria da Gloria had recruited her in Laguna. Now in Nice *she* recruited, with Peppino recruiting 100 Red Shirts.

She and Peppino had to find their battle. After six days with Peppino in Nice, leaving the children in Donna Rosa's care, with Andrea Aguyar beside her and Mr. Anzani, the Deiderys and of course Peppino--she took a boat to Genoa.

She guided Garibaldi in the flesh to the Genovese people who'd shouted Vivas! for him months earlier. Somehow news of his coming always preceded him.

The 100 Red Shirts recruited in Nice had to be outfitted. The forgery she'd arranged deep in the night was a requisition for supplies, signed by His Excellency, governor of Genoa, presented now to Genoa's city prefect: "400 hats, boot covers and vests; 400 cloth overpants; 500 overcoats; 500 rifles with gunpowder and bayonets; 25 officers swords; munitions and gunpowder caps."

A banquet was held in Garibaldi's honor. He gave a speech:

"We must make every effort to chase the Austrians from this land without becoming engaged in a war likely to last two or three years. Let's banish the thought of political systems, let's not argue about forms of government, let's not create parties. Men, arms, money--that's what we need. I was a Republican but when I learned King Charles Albert was championing the cause, I pledged allegiance to follow his flag. In him I see hope for independence."

She'd never heard him in such exalted circumstances, his voice sweeping, echoing around the hall and cheered by hundreds. But Young Italians exchanged looks of disapproval--they supported a united front with the Piedmont monarchists against Austria but felt Garibaldi was too enthusiastic about King Charles Albert.

In Genoa, Mr. Anzani took to sick bed, Giacomo Medici beside him. Anzani said: "Do not be too hard on Garibaldi. He's a man of destiny. A great part of Italy's future depends on him. It will be a grave error to abandon him."

Francesco Anzani's wooden coffin was carried through Liguria and Lombardy to Alzate and laid to rest in the grave of his ancestors.

"I've never known a more capable and honorable man or soldier of loftier character." She was with Garibaldi when he also said, "The Mazzinians tormented him to use his influence with me."

The children needed one of them. She returned to Nice. Peppino and Aguyar traveled north to meet King Charles Albert in his royal headquarters at Roverbello, near Mantua, five miles from the battlefront.

She should be more conventional, play up to her mother-in-law somewhat--after all, Donna Rosa cared for the children.

"You should have heard your son in front of the people of Genoa--" Donna Rosa and Padrone Domenico had sprung from the ancient republic--"Now he's on his way to meet with King Charles Albert. Your son to meet with the king..."

"My son was raised to obey his parents and honor his king."

Communications was more facile in Italy than in Uruguay. Old friends of Peppino's like sea captain Carpenetto, trusted officers like Captain Origoni who'd helped organize the Italian Legion in Montevideo brought her news. As always, Peppino wrote to her.

His feelings were strange, waiting in the Palazzo Benato, Roverbello, near Mantua, few miles from the front lines--he was about to meet the man who 14 years earlier had sentenced him to death for desertion and high treason. After being shuffled from one minister to another--Italian red tape could fill the vast, virgin plains of Uruguay!-- Giuseppe Maria Garibaldi of Piedmont was led into his king's royal sala.

"I and the Italian Legion offer you our loyal service. I request you entrust to me the rank of general."

King Charles Albert thanked Garibaldi in behalf of the Italian people for his services to Montevideo. "Go to the war office in Turin. Minister Ricci will arrange for you and your men to serve." After the meeting, the king wrote to Minister Ricci:

"I hasten to warn you that I have today received in audience the famous General Garibaldi, who has come from South America and arrived in Genoa where he left 60 of his disciples whom he offered to me along with himself. The antecedents of these gentlemen, and particularly of the self-styled general, make it absolutely impossible for us to accept them in the army, and particularly to make Garibaldi a general. If there was a naval war, he might be employed as a leader of privateers, but to employ him otherwise would be to dishonor the army. As I think he will be coming to Turin, where he will not lack supporters, be ready for the attack. The best would be if they went off to any other place; and to encourage him and his brave fellows, they might be given a subsidy on the condition that they go away."

In her short, glorious life, King Charles Albert of Piedmont joined Montevidean Minister-of-war Francesco Vidal and Argentine dictator Manuel de Rosas in infamy.

Peppino was made to wait again outside the war office in Turin, Andrea Aguyar patiently beside him. She and the children were safe in Nice--Garibaldi was King of Nice!

Minister Ricci didn't mince words. "You ought to go to Venice. There they will give you some small ship and you can ply your trade as a buccaneer. That's your place. There's none for you here."

"I'm a bird of freedom and not for a cage."

Peppino paced under the arcades, Aguyar standing quietly in shadows. Giacomo Medici found them. A thousand recruits had been raised in Viareggio, Lucca.

"These people aren't worthy of submission of hearts like ours."

Medici suggested they leave for Milan that night.

Milan's revolutionary committee appointed Garibaldi general in the Lombard army but gave him a desk job, recruiting and organizing volunteers. General of Desk! He summoned the legionaries from Genoa, then confined himself to bed with a fever.

Medici applied for arms to General Salasco, Charles Albert's military governor in Milan.

Salasco: "It would be a waste of arms. Garibaldi is a *sciabalatore*--brave soldier and good swordsman but a poor general."

Medici said they would find their own arms but needed uniforms, Red Shirts.

"The Red Shirt makes the Legion too conspicuous, endangering the others. No uniforms."

They had to have uniforms. She wasn't in Milan to organize the women to cut, sew 500 Red Shirts. Reluctant Salasco opened the Austrian stores--plenty of white cloth. Legionaries from Genoa made a sort of white blouse. Medici reported to Garibaldi: "We look like cooks."

Peppino was ordered to Bergamo to train new recruits. The move was really a diversion for the main army--there would be no time to train new recruits. The Legion, called the "Anzani Battalion" now, marched to Bergamo. Before they were able to eat, they were ordered to return to Milan by forced march.

Taking the offensive against Radetsky's famous quadrangle of forts, King Charles Albert and his forces were defeated in the hills of Somma-Campagna, near Custoza, then massacred at Gaito and Volta. Charles Albert surrendered Milan, disbanded the royal army, entered negotiations with Austria for an armistice.

Instead of returning to Milan, Garibaldi marched to Monza.

Radetsky sent General D'Aspre with 7,000 to find and destroy the Anzani Battalion.

Garibaldi ordered Medici to round up deserters from the king's army. Garibaldi wrote to Venice's inspired leader, Jewish lawyer Daniele Manin:

We've heard of Charles Albert's capitulation and the evacuation of Milan. All this has nothing to do with us. The Italian war against Austria will continue.

Her husband was continuing the war against Austria himself, a people's army along the Alpine slopes, troops based in neutral territory then raiding across the Swiss border, retreating back into Switzerland. Mountainous country, as Garibaldi had learned in Rio Grande, was suitable for fighting guerrilla warfare. The Anzani Battalion entered the mountainous country of the Italian lakes.

Mazzini himself seized a musket, joined the battalion and carried a standard that read: "God and the People." From now on Mazzini signed his articles and proclamations: "Mazzini, soldier of Garibaldi's Legion."

Warrior Garibaldi watched Spirit Mazzini--the frail, inspiring lawyer, arch conspirator, founder of Young Italy and Young Europe struggling to keep up in the rain.

Proclaimed commander-in-chief of the Italian People's Army, Garibaldi immediately requested all leaders of volunteer corps still fighting and scattered in Lombardy--Luciano Manara, Durando, Griffin--to contact him. Such contacts didn't come. Anzani Battalion of 500 wandered north through Sesto Calende, reached Castelelto on Piedmont's side of the Ticino River. Peppino wrote to his wife:

"On this occasion I revived the hope I've nurtured for many years of inciting our fellow citizens to that partisan warfare which, in the absence of an organized army, could lead to the general arming of the nation, if the nation really has an inner and resolute wish to redeem itself."

Medici recruited a few hundred, raising the corps to 800, enough to take the field against Austria. On August 12 ('48), a proclamation signed G. Garibaldi appeared on village walls in Florence, Venice, Turin and Rome:

"If the King of Piedmont has a crown he wishes to save by guilt and cowardice, my companions and I don't wish to save our lives by infamy and to abandon, without sacrificing ourselves, our sacred soil to the victory of those who oppress and ravage it."

King Charles Albert ordered the author arrested and brought to trial, and sent a force under his brother, Duke of Genoa, to round up Garibaldi and his men. So the enemy, Radetsky, had sent a force against Peppino, now his own king.

Garibaldi continued north toward Lago Maggiore, in Arona served a requisition notice on the town clerk: "1,286 rations of bread, 20 sacks of rice, 3 sacks of oats for the small number of horses, 7,000 lire in cash."

Then as now the Italian lakes surrounded by mountains were a popular holiday resort. Steamships *Verbaro* and *San Carlo* navigated on Lago Maggiore. Garibaldi seized them, embarked the men and steamed past villas on the lake's west side, their balconies filled with waving, cheering women.

"Lovely faces and so animated it seemed they wished to fly in order to welcome the brave men who don't despair of snatching their hearts from the oppressor."

In Luino, small town seven miles from the Swiss border, Garibaldi stopped at the Beccaria Inn. Overcome by fatigue, running a fever, he really had to have a couple of hours' rest. He told Medici to keep an eye on everything.

Half hour later, Austrian troops approached Beccaria Inn.

Garibaldi was on the march cross country to Varese.

700 Croat infantry under General Molinary overpowered Garibaldi's rearguard, captured Beccaria Inn.

Garibaldi turned back--recapturing the inn would achieve a moral victory. A unit of Pavese cavalry stormed the inn and retook it, leaving one officer and three line soldiers dead, 33 prisoners.

Luino's citizens made no attempt to help. They'd rushed to the lake, stood there, watched the battle. Luino wasn't Montevideo.

One of the women stepped up. Signora Montegazza, hearing the firing, crossed the lake in her private boat. She took care of the wounded on both sides.

A town official had given information for money. Without taking his cigar out of his mouth, Garibaldi ordered Medici to shoot the informer. Medici blew out his brains.

Garibaldi sent the seriously wounded to a hospital in Cannibio, held prisoners in the two steamers, left 60 men to guard the boats. With 500 he set off again for Varese.

The battalion marched up, down mountains between Lagos Maggiore and Como in weather hot as it was in Salto. Peppino drew up his black silk scarf. She received a letter:

"Mazzini joined us on the march, continued with us as far as Como. From Como he crossed into Switzerland while I was making preparations to hold the country in the Comaschi Mountains. Many of his followers, or pretended followers, followed him onto foreign soil. This naturally encouraged others to desert."

Desertions notwithstanding, the column reached the heights overlooking Varese. Three Austrian columns began an encircling movement designed to cut off retreat into Piedmont and Switzerland.

Medici took 68 men and formed a line in three villages on slopes of the San Maffei Mountains, left flank near the Swiss border. Deep in the black night, one section deserted. At dawn an Austrian column attacked.

Medici resisted until his last cartridge was spent--four hours. Led by a Swiss guide, Medici and 60 retreated to Lugano, Switzerland.

Garibaldi and his troops fortified themselves inside the small hill town Morazzone, south of Varese; cut off, surrounded by the second Austrian column of 4,000, who set fire to the houses on the town's outskirts. Morazzone burned throughout the night. At dawn the Austrian column attacked.

Garibaldi held out all day with 400, one cavalry detachment, 18 artillery guns. With the settling in of the black night, color of her hair, and fires burning low, Garibaldi formed his men in close column, then they threw themselves on the enemy with bayonets, forging passage through the line. One hour from Morazzone, in the open country, Garibaldi disbanded the troops--make their way into Switzerland best way they could.

Garibaldi walked. Disguised as a peasant, he walked through Luino, took a steamer across the lake and walked 16 hours along mountain footpaths into Switzerland.

Medici found him three days later in bed in an inn near Lugano, burning with fever and his legs swollen.

"I've had a walk, a long walk. Is your company ready?"

"We have 60 men."

"Very well. Let's have one night's sleep and then tomorrow we'll rally the men and begin afresh."

Tomorrow turned out to be one year later.

Ill, Garibaldi moved to the estate of Milanese patriot Marchese de Rosales and his young beautiful lover, Contessa dal Varme. The Contessa had left her pro-Austrian husband and eloped with the Marchese--they'd been imprisoned together. The Contessa received a letter:

"The interest you're taking in my unfortunate husband can have been dictated only by a well-shaped soul and well-born heart. Therefore I profit by your kindness to beg you to give the enclosed letter to my husband. I hope you will dispose of me at any time and in any place in which I may be of some usefulness to you and, pray, believe me, your most humble servant, Anita Garibaldi."

The Contessa's fair, young hands handed Peppino a letter:

"From your note of 26th last, we've learned of your reverses. I'd been expecting it for some time, because I couldn't understand how a handful of soldiers could stand up to an entire army. The only action you can take is to come home to your family and wait for a more auspicious time. This, my dearest, is the only advice I can give you. Our children are very well, don't forget them. Mother embraces you. Love me as I love you and believe me, your most affectionate wife."

In Nice, morning of September 10, good friend Deidery handed her a passport with the name "Risso".

Peppino stood there, beard shaven, hair short, drawn, ill. He took to sick bed. She cared for him three weeks.

Resistance to Austria continued in Lombardy. Daniele Manin was holding out in Venice. In the South, King Ferdinand had revoked Naples' constitution and was attacking the revolution in Sicily, bombing civilians of Messina and earning himself the nickname, "King Bomba". Dressed in civilian clothes, passport with the name "Risso", and leaving the children with the Deiderys, she and Peppino left Nice by mail coach, destination Genoa.

32. MR. & MRS RISSO

Three times she touched on Genoa, land of her husband's ancestors--Peppino's father springing from Chiavari of a family of shipbuilders, his mother from Loano of fisherfolk. No matter the name on her passport, she was recognized--"La bella Braziliana!" A small crowd surged around their horses, led them to the relay station.

Peppino spoke at a rally:

"Rise up with the rights you don't hold, of the blood you've shed and of the glorious name Italy that you've heard derided by the enemy. Rise up as men geared for death. To naught else ask for victory but to god and your sword. Place your faith not in symbols but in justice. He who wants to win can win."

Over the next weeks of autumn, she recruited and listened to revolutionaries request her and Peppino to come to their cities' aid. Peppino accepted every invitation. As in Salto, she didn't have a clue what was on his mind. Peppino was waiting. She waited.

Pellegrino Rossi

Sicilian revolutionary Paolo Fabrizi told them King Ferdinand of Naples, supported by Pius IX and his prime minister Pellegrino Rossi, had destroyed Messina and Palermo with bombs, without respect to gender or sex. The Sicilian people had risen with force of arms--rebels in place, as in Laguna.

On November 24, she, Aguyar, Peppino, 38 legionaries from Montevideo and 72 new recruits took the French steamer *Pharamond,* destination Sicily. Autumn's new gold crowned the Tuscan hills, mountain range white.

"Look, Peppino--snow!"

"Marble, my darling, white Carrera marble."

Eight o'clock next morning, the *Pharamond* stopped at Livorno for supplies. She detoured from Sicily. Her husband and son and one Thousand other volunteers completed the expedition 11 years later.

In Livorno the crowd cheered and waved tricolors at the waterfront, *Via Grande* and the piazza decorated as if for a holiday. Tuscany's revolutionary army wanted Garibaldi to take command.

"We're on our way to Sicily."

They would be helping the Sicilians by leading Tuscany's army across the southern frontier, through the papal states and into the Kingdom of Naples, attacking King Ferdinand in the rear. She and Peppino agreed to stay in Livorno a few days.

Telegrams flew back and forth between Livorno and Prime Minister Montanelli in Florence:

Livorno: Garibaldi, although intending to go to Sicily, wouldn't be opposed to offering his services to the Tuscan government. Please advise. He leaves this afternoon.

Montanelli: Ministry not constituted yet. If possible ask him to delay departure.

Disturbances broke out--coaches overturned, fires, windows smashed.

Livorno: People of Livorno want Garibaldi remain in Tuscany, whatever terms. Have succeeded in delaying departure until seven. Must have reply at once. Population out of control.

Montanelli didn't reply. Garibaldi himself sent a telegram:

"I want to know if you are placing Garibaldi in command of Tuscany's forces to work against Bourbons. Yes or no?"

Still Montanelli didn't reply.

That evening the *Pharamond* embarked for Sicily, she and Peppino not on board. They were at the theater.

An emissary representing Daniele Manin of Venice urged them to come to the ancient republic's aid. Peppino accepted.

With great speed, Minister Montanelli gave her and Peppino leave to recruit, promised all assistance to get them on their way east across the border. "They're like a plague of locusts. Let's do all we can to get them away quickly, so that they infest as few places as possible."

She and Peppino recruited 300--300 new children. They requisitioned 300 overcoats, 300 pair of boots, 250 muskets and bayonets, 20 officers' sabers. Their plan now was to march across Tuscany and the papal states to the Adriatic, embark at Ravenna for Venice.

She would spend the rest of her short, glorious life trying to get to Venice.

She took one of Italy's first trains, with Peppino traveling to Florence in order to persuade Tuscany's government to send its army to Milan. She and Peppino stayed in the house of his boyhood friend Carlo Notari. From the balcony Peppino gave a speech:

"The Tuscan government shouldn't merely be pushed. It should be forced and whipped along. Forced by demonstrations, I mean. Italy can choose one of two ways with her rulers: overthrow them or drag them along. There's no middle way. It's one thing or the other."

The speech didn't produce one recruit. Tuscany didn't send its army to Milan and didn't fulfill the requisition. Instead, Tuscany withdrew the Legion's rations.

She raised money for rations.

Her eyes took in Florence's sites famous then as now. First time in her life she had her hair cut by a hairdresser, short do. This time *her* hair was cut short but she was still jealous, now over Elizabeth Barret Browning--English women did seem to take to Peppino--who gave him a poem:

"If we did not fight exactly
We fired muskets in the air
To show that victory was ours of right."

The march to Ravenna would be difficult, Apennine

Mountains in winter. One of them had to be with the children. She went, returning to Nice.

Peppino with 100 marched high in the Apennines knee-deep in snow. The cold was bitter. Her recruits had no cloaks, only make-shift garments, some in rags. At the frontier of the papal states, 400 of the pope's Swiss mercenaries blocked their passage, the way back to Tuscany also blocked. Garibaldi found an inn. The friendly innkeeper allowed the men to crowd in, bivouac on the floor.

Barnabite friar Ugo Bassi lead a rally in front of Bologna's *le due torri:*

"Garibaldi is squeezed in our mountains between two armies sent not by our General Zucchi but by the pope through his prime minister Pellegrino Rossi, who sent Zucchi this telegram--'Get rid of Garibaldi as soon as possible. That is--crush him!' Choose now-- Garibaldi or Pius IX! Italy or continued slavery!"

"Garibaldi! Italy! Garibaldi! Italy!"

Mothers offered their sons. A young girl stepped forward holding locks of her hair. She had nothing else to give to Italy's war except her hair.

The fired crowd marched to General Zucchi's headquarters. The general came out.

"Either our brothers come here or you come down from that balcony."

Father Alessandro Gavazzi, recruiter for the Legion in Bologna, demanded withdrawal of the Swiss mercenaries, threatening an uprising.

Garibaldi entered Bologna alone, was escorted in state amid thunderous cheering to the *Grande Albergo Reale*. Ugo Bassi greeted him wearing a wooden cross over a Red Shirt. From then on, the patriot priest was Legion chaplain.

Wealthy Bolognese radical Angelo Masina presented himself and cavalry battalion of lancers. Garibaldi reviewed the eager, young men elegantly mounted on splendid horses.

On to Ravenna, she followed them--Father Ugo Bassi, Angelo Masina and his Lancers marching with the battalion. Ravenna was on the verge of revolution, and the battalion's arrival added to the excitement. Ravenna impressed Garibaldi. Its people were taciturn, cool, undemonstrative. He was in the crowd in the public square when a police informant, in full view of hundreds, was assassinated. Not one citizen gave a statement.

The government insisted Garibaldi leave for Venice at once. He would leave when the contingent from Mantua arrived, he told General de la Tour.

General de la Tour was prepared to use force, his troops outside town armed with two cannon.

If the Legion was attacked, they would fight.

Dr. Nino Bonnet, one of Ravenna's leading citizens, rode through the night distributing arms to the revolutionary national guard.

Then incredible news arrived from Rome--Prime Minister

Pellegrino Rossi had been assassinated! Pius IX had fled to Naples!

Margaret Fuller, North America's first female correspondent in Italy, wrote home to her mother in Boston: "For me, I never thought to have heard of a violent act with satisfaction; but this act affected me as one of terrible justice."

She'd marched in a torchlight procession in Montevideo, so hopeful of the new pope's liberal leanings. But then Romans wanted more than limited franchise regarding property, an upper house composed of clerics nominated by the pope; if a decree passed that house, it was subject to veto by the cardinals. Rome's constitution had been granted under duress, so he really hadn't granted it--Pius IX had lost control. His refusal to join the war against Austria led to violent reaction from all classes: lawyers, journalists, students, parliamentarians, artists, royalty, the poor of Trastevere led by the burly wine merchant Angelo Brunetti, nicknamed "Ciceruacchio". Pius appointed Pellegrino Rossi prime minister--strong layman who would protect his positions. Tall, thin, haughty, Roman aristocrat, Count Pellegrino Rossi was in total sympathy with Pius' refusal to send troops north and insisted on preserving the pope's temporal powers, assisted and supported King Ferdinand's bombardment of Messina's citizens, and arrested and sent back refugees from Naples and Sicily to imprisonment and torture. On November 15, Rossi went to address the pope's new parliament in the *Palazzo della Cancelleria*, law and order speech. The prime minister was handed a message of warning. He treated criticism with contempt.

"So much the worse for them if they carry out their plans. Rome cannot wait."

Rossi began climbing the palace steps. Ciceruacchio's son Luigi plunged a knife in his back. Pellegrino Rossi fell dead across the palace steps. The next day the crowd stormed the pope's palace, killing His confessor. Nine days later, Pius IX fled Rome disguised as the Bavarian minister's servant. King "Bomba" of Naples received His Holiness with great honor in his palace at Gaeta.

She knew Peppino would go to Rome.

He turned the march south--Cesena, Macerata, then Rieti, staying close to the Adriatic. Garibaldi and Aguyar took a different route to Rieti, spying out the land along the Neapolitan frontier--scene of fighting when the Neapolitan forces would invade the papal states.

In Rieti, halfway to Rome, Peppino billeted himself and staff in the 18th-century palace of Marchese Geralamo Colelli, Peppino taking a modest room on the top floor. She received a letter from Rieti. Peppino wrote that artisans, shopkeepers, laborers, bandits, convicts, 14- and 15-year-old boys joined what he called now "The First Italian Legion." Italian Legion-Red Shirts-Anzani Battalion-First Italian Legion. An incident in Cesena had saddened him. Two officers who'd fought with them in Montevideo, Ramorino and Risso, whose passport they'd used, fought a duel--Risso was killed.

"I would have expelled from the Legion the officer who took a blow from anyone."

In Rome, a Junta composed of Carabinieri and National Guard assumed temporary power and ordered election of a Constituent Assembly on the basis of universal suffrage. The Eternal City became the first in Italy to achieve democratic self-government. Nearly half the adult population of Rome flocked to the polls with joy and enthusiasm. Posters plastered all over the Eternal City read: "Anyone Who Votes Is Ex-communicated."

Ciceruacchio replied with a procession burlesquing catholic sacraments, men and women in red hats.

From King Ferdinand's palace in Gaeta, exiled Pius IX wrote to heads of state of France, Spain, Austria: "I appeal to you to suppress the new Roman Republic with force of arms."

French general Cavaignac assembled 3,000 troops and ships in Marseilles, made ready to sail.

The people of Macerata elected Garibaldi to Rome's Constituent Assembly.

Garibaldi, Aguyar and Angelo Masina took a mail coach to Rome for inauguration of its National Assembly. The Hall was packed. Racked by arthritis, Garibaldi had to be carried in, by Aguyar, both wearing the Red Shirt. They sat in the rear, listened awhile. Garibaldi asked for the floor.

"Forms and ceremonials can do little for the destiny of the Italian nation. The vital question now is one of principles. Delay of even one minute is a crime when one-third of the population remains enslaved. I truly believe that, the other form of government having ceased to be, what is best for Rome today is a Republic. Long live the Republic!"

Spectators in the gallery erupted with applause.

But Garibaldi encountered indecisiveness and unwillingness on the part of the regular army chiefs to recognize him and the Legion, leaving Rome with rank of lieutenant-colonel of the Roman army, authority to maintain an army of no more than 500, no stores or cloaks, and instructions to defend Porto San Georgio on the Adriatic against whom he didn't know.

Four days later, evening of February 9 (1849), Roman citizens held a mass rally at the Apollo Theater. "Republic! Republic! Republic!" Next day the Assembly's eleven deputies passed the Fundamental Statute of four Articles:

Article 1. The Papacy is deposed in fact and in law from temporal government of the Roman State.

Article 2. The Roman Pontiff will be granted all the guarantees necessary for his independence in the exercise of his spiritual power.

Article 3. Form of government of the Roman State will be a complete democracy and will take the glorious name "The Roman Republic."

Article 4. The Roman Republic will have with the rest of Italy such relationship as will lead to a common nationality.

Mazzini was declared citizen of the Republic. He arrived in

Rome. The Assembly established a triumvirate, Mazzini the most powerful. She received another letter from Subiaco:

"I must hear from you. Tell me what you think of events in Genoa and Livorno... With what contempt you must look on this generation of hermaphrodites whom I've so often tried to make noble, with such little result. I'm ashamed to belong to a family which has so many cowards."

33. REUNION IN RIETI

She suffered the presentiment Peppino was in grave danger, experienced the gravity of desperation he'd experienced following the shipwreck in Laguna--life without Peppino was insupportable. She had to go to him. Once again she left the children in Donna Rosa's care.

She had enough money for the boat fare to Genoa. Fourth time she touched in Genoa, land of Peppino's ancestors. She borrowed 200 francs from Carpenetto, Peppino's good old friend. Men were angels in situations of this kind. Her coach sped through the winter of central Italy, cold, rain--the coach roof was a gift from heaven--flying past clustered cypresses, colossal pines of the Umbrian Hills and ancient villages clinging to slopes.

She surprised Peppino, walking nonchalantly through his modest room's open door. He needed her now more than ever.

Marchese Collelli had horses, a liveried carriage drawn by white mares. The Marchese marveled at the sight of her riding out in the early evening beside her husband. She and Peppino visited ruins, medieval castles. It was Good Friday. A procession of the Fraternity of the Good Death, cross shrouded in black, marched with lighted taper to the church of St. Augustine. Peppino dismounted, took off his hat. She remained mounted, hat on.

In Rieti she met and befriended friar Ugo Bassi, Legion chaplain, marking him for a glorious death. She met Dr. Ripari, Legion doctor, who 11 years later would be one of the Thousand in Sicily who remembered her. She organized a first-aid station. The Legion was short of muskets, munitions. She negotiated with blacksmiths for pikes, lances. Rieti's blacksmiths forged lances. Every legionary went armed.

Peppino was silent several days. Morning of April 3 he bolted awake with the impulse to write to Mazzini. She was beside him.

"Brother Mazzini,

"This has no other object than to bring you greetings, and I write with my own hand. May Providence support you on your brilliant but arduous career and enable you to carry out all there is in your mind, to the benefit of the country. Remember that in Rieti are to

be found your friends in the faith, and they are unchangeable. G.Garibaldi."

On April 24, 9,000 French troops arrived in Civitavecchia commanded by General Oudinot, devout catholic, son of Napoleon I's Marshal. King Ferdinand prepared to invade from the south, as Garibaldi and Aguyar had foretold. Small Spanish fleet and 9,000 Spanish troops joined the King of Naples. Marshal Radetsky crushed King Charles Albert then swept south, taking Ferrara, Bologna and bombing Genoa when she wasn't there. Charles Albert retired to Portugal after abdicating in favor of his son, Victor Emanuel II.

Oudinot sent a message to Mazzini: "The French will enter Rome but they come as friends, wishing only to protect Rome from Austrian intervention and to restore peace between the pope and his subjects."

Mazzini appointed a Military Commission of Defense. Ciceruacchio set up Committees of the Barricades in every quarter. As in Montevideo, citizens threw up barricades. Women spread sand on the streets so that cavalry horses could have surer footing. Princess Belgiojoso formed the Committee of Ambulances, organizing medical assistance, transforming the Quirinal, the pope's palace, to a hospital. Mazzini appointed General Avezzana Minister of War. Avezzana had fought in the Spanish Revolutionary War, Mexico, and knew Garibaldi and appointed him General of Brigade. Avezzana dispatched to him the urgent message: "At this hour we have reason to believe that the French, intending to restore the pope's temporal power, have landed 6,000 troops in Civitavecchia and are sending 1,000 more to Ancona. We must bring all our forces together. We request that upon receiving this dispatch you start immediately for Rome."

She would go first, find quarters. She purchased a coach ticket for Rome. But she raised a fever, ran her hand over her stomach. *This baby would definitely be born in Italy.* In Peppino's silence and expression on his face, she read his concern. She negotiated again-- she'd return to Nice on the condition Peppino made arrangements for her arrival as soon as he was inside Rome.

She was leaving her heart with him, she told Peppino.

That night over a glass of wine, the Marchese Colleli: "Garibaldi, you're a very lucky man. Anita is the most exquisite woman I've ever known. And how she loves you."

That faraway look came over Peppino's face. "I love her more than I can say."

She stopped in Genoa to pay the 200 francs to Carpenetto. Once in Nice, she didn't unpack. She began sewing a silk dress and fashionable hat--outfit fit for a rich lady of Spain.

34. ROME

She didn't see action on the Janiculum, highest of Rome's hills but her statue stands there--she's mounted, holding baby, free arm raised firing her gun, looking out over the best of men, women and children dying gloriously for country, across the valley of vineyards, dome of St. Peter's and distant hill valleys.

One hour of one's life in Rome was worth a century of life.

Military bands played and distant bugles sounded, everywhere flags and cockades. Rome was filled with soldiers in brilliant uniforms decorated with braid, flashes and gilt, swords clanking against cobblestones. The Republic's armed forces consisted of 1,400 Roman volunteers; 1,000 national guardsmen; 450 university students with no military training; 300 volunteer civil servants of the taxation department; 2,500 carabinieri of the old papal civil guard.

Suddenly, 6 p.m., April 25, 1849, after a forced marched from Rieti in a rain storm, 1,300 new soldiers the likes of which Romans in all their glorious history had never seen rode slowly through the main gate, Porta Maggiore.

"Garibaldi has come!" traveled up and down the Corso.

They were gaunt and untidy, long untrimmed hair, unkempt beards, knees bare, tanned by the sun, covered with dust. A few Red Shirts here and there but mainly they wore ill-fitting, navy-blue trousers with belts holding knives, black Calabrian hats with broad brims and high crowns stuck with long black feathers. A few carried muskets, most carried lances. Her Peppino rode in their midst in a Red Shirt, white poncho with scarlet lining and black felt hat with feathers, her colorful handkerchief knotted around his neck.

"Isn't he beautiful?"

Andrea Aguyar, jet black on jet black charger, rode beside Garibaldi.

"What soldiers are these?"

"Garibaldini."

Dutch artist J.P. Koelman described Garibaldi enter Rome:

"...broad-shouldered, with a massive chest, light chestnut hair falling over his shoulders, a big mustache and light reddish-brown beard ending in two points, his face red with the sun. The most striking feature of all is the nose with its broad base, which makes one think of a lion, a similarity which, according to his soldiers, is even more noticeable when his eyes flash and his sable hair streams from his forehead like a mane."

Garibaldi took his first drink in Rome, water, not from her *bequina* but from a well. Provisions hadn't been made for billeting the troops.

"There must be a dead animal at the bottom of the well!"

Garibaldi and Aguyar rode up to the vast convent of *San Silvestro* and gave the nuns one hour to leave. Within the hour, soldiers streamed in and rested on bundles of straw on the floor. Some rifled through drawers and found love letters, babies attire, instruments of erotic use.

Determined to keep Rome a respectable place, Mazzini transferred Garibaldi and his men to slum quarters in Trastevere. Garibaldi took a room in a tenement, Via delle Carozze 59.

Early next morning until high noon, raising his black silk scarf in Rome while she cared for the children in Nice, Peppino studied the light and terrain. The French had 40,000 soldiers. Rome's walls and fortifications were 18 miles in circumference. They didn't have enough men to hold so long a line. The western boundary was the wall built in the 17th century, running from St. Peter's and the Vatican to the Janiculum, down to the city gate Porta San Pancrazio and on toward the south. East of the Janiculum, inside the city, the ground fell sharply past the ancient Aurelean Wall of the 3rd century and down to Trastevere, behind which flowed the Tiber. West of the Janiculum, outside the walls, spread the gardens of three residential villas, vacated now, their entrances adjacent to a small villa, the Vascello. Ground inside the gardens gently sloped 250 yards to the top of a ridge nearly as high as the Janiculum. On this ridge stood the tall, four-story Villa Corsini, also called *Casina dei Quattri Venti,* House of the Four Winds, because of its exposed position. The French mustn't occupy the Corsini and its gardens. If they establish cannon on the Corsini's ridge, they could bombard the Janiculum and main gate and cover the area between gardens and walls. On April 29, Garibaldi took possession of the villas and gardens and established headquarters in the Villa Corsini.

Next morning, spectacular sunrise over Rome, he watched

over the valley of vineyards, dome of St. Peter's and distant hill valleys. He had 2,500, including the 450 university students, Colonel Galetti with 1,800, Colonel Masi with 2,000 in reserve.

General Oudinot advanced with 7,000 infantry and full complement of field guns, vanguard marching straight for the summit of Vatican Hill crowned by an old, round tower.

"Italians can't fight," French officers told their soldiers.

Montevideo all over again, this time without her at the outset.

At noon, a sentry on St. Peter's walls saw French columns approaching. Other sentries on the wall beat the drums, broken beat of the alarm. Bells rang from campaniles of hundreds of churches.

Garibaldi ordered artillery gunners to open fire on Oudinot's feint attack on Porta Cavallegieri.

"The midday gun," a French officer told Oudinot.

Garibaldi followed with a round of grapeshot, musket fire. Soldiers fell dead around General Oudinot.

The French fell back behind dikes and mounds, fired at the ramparts overhead, climbed up on spike nails.

Garibaldi waved in the 450 university students of no military experience. They stormed through the gardens, fought with bayonets among flowering rosebushes. The French reeled. After an hour of hand-to-hand fighting, reinforcements drove the students back along the sunken lane north of the gardens.

Garibaldi sent in Galletti and his 1,800, keeping Masi's men in reserve.

Garibaldi rode forward, saber drawn--"With bayonets!"

The French broke, retreating in disorder. They lost 500 killed and wounded, Angelo Masina took 350 prisoners. The defenders lost 200 killed, one prisoner--Ugo Bassi had been captured administering Extreme Unction.

Garibaldi had been hit in the side. He sent Dr. Ripari a note from the field: "Come to me after dark. I've been wounded but nobody must know." Aguyar found his companion's saddle soaked with blood. Neck, wrists, side--she found Peppino with wounds. His side wound, treated at night in his room, caused pain and discomfort the next two months of constant combat.

That night all Rome was illuminated, every window burned a candle. Happy crowds filled streets, cafes, piazzas; treated the French prisoners with drinks and cigars, showed them around St. Peter's and the monuments, then released them.

Not to be undone by a "bunch of radicals," General Oudinot released the garrison he'd taken at Civitavecchia and his one prisoner, Ugo Bassi.

Daybreak next morning, Garibaldi made a sortie in force outside the city--strike the French before they reach their ships.

Mazzini ordered Garibaldi back to Rome--a crushing defeat would imperil prospects for conciliation. Mazzini preferred expelling Neapolitan troops from Roman territory.

General Oudinot settled in Civitavecchia, waited for

reinforcements.

King Ferdinand lead his army of 10,000 into the Alban Hills near the ancient Volcian city of Velletri, 25 miles south of Rome.

In the dead of black night, Garibaldi marched out with 2,300: the Legion, university students, a few dragoons, Luciano Manara's aristocratic Lombard Brigade. Going against an army four times larger, Garibaldi decided against a frontal attack on the Alban Hills, at the same time had to prevent advance on Rome--they'd threaten, keep Ferdinand's right flank engaged. The night march proceeded to Palestrina, feinting first in another direction crossed the plain toward Tivoli she would see, and next day camped in the grounds of Hadrian's villa she would visit with the women of Tivoli among orange groves and fig trees.

Luciano Manara recorded his first contact with Garibaldi in the field: "I'm going with Garibaldi. He is a devil, a panther. His men are a troop of brigands, and I am going to support their mad onrush with my disciplined, silent, gentlemanly regiment."

One month later Luciano Manara was Garibaldi's chief of staff.

Manara's friend Emilio Dandolo, gentleman of the Brigade, watched camp go up, the way she'd encamped in the vast, virgin pampas, camp life a pastime for her:

"...the numerous fires which glistened among the ruins, and lighted up their subterraneous caverns, produced a strange and picturesque effect. The singular aspect of the camp seemed in unison with the wildness of the scene." Garibaldi and his staff were dressed in scarlet blouses and hats of all kinds, without pretension to military ornament. They rode on American saddles. Followed by their South American orderlies, they hurried back and forth, now dispensing, then collecting--active, rapid, tireless. "When the troops halted to decamp, or to rest, while the soldiers piled their arms we used to be surprised to see officers, Garibaldi himself included, leap down from their horses and attend to the wants of their own steeds. Then they unrolled their own saddles, which were made to be unrolled and form a small kind of tent..." Three or four colonels and majors jumped onto their horses, armed with long lassoes set out at full speed in search of sheep and oxen. When they had collected enough from the Cardinals' great estates, they returned, driving their flocks before them. The herd was divided among the companies, and then all, indiscriminately--officers and men--fell to, killing, cutting up, and roasting at enormous fires quarters of oxen, kids, young pigs.

"Garibaldi in the meanwhile," wrote Dandolo, "lay stretched out under his tent. If, on the other hand, the enemy were at hand, he remained constantly on horseback, giving orders and visiting the outposts. Often, disguised as a peasant, he risked his own safety in daring reconnaissances, but most frequently he passed whole hours examining the environs with the aid of his telescope. The order to march was arranged on the preceding day, and the corps set out without anyone knowing where they might arrive the day after. Owing to his patriarchal simplicity, Garibaldi appeared more like the chief of a tribe of Indians than a general. At the approach of danger, and in the heat of combat, the rapidity of his movements is astonishing."

The chief directed the march south toward the great road leading from Rome to Naples, on May 7 camping under cover of night amid Palestrina's great ruins at the foot of the Sabine Hills, directly opposite the Alban Hills where King Ferdinand of Naples was camped. Garibaldi ordered the Lombard Brigade to camp in the Augustinian monastery. The monks refused to let in the Brigade. Manara, Dandolo waited under pouring rain. Garibaldi blew the monastery door. The Brigade took possession.

Over the next few days, Garibaldi sent out detachments of 30 to 60 men, who scoured the undulating plain and wooded mountain between Valmontone and Friscati. One detachment under Ugo Bassi was driven back by Neapolitan troops advancing on Palestrina.

Ugo Bassi rode out:

"We are Italians, we mustn't fight one another, we're fighting for the same thing--our country, our Italy!"

A large force of Neapolitans--drive away the bandit!--advanced on Palestrina in two columns.

From the old fortress Castel San Pietro atop the mountain behind Palestrina, Garibaldi and staff officers watched the columns wind toward them by two parallel roads one mile apart. Garibaldi attacked, rushing down the steep cobbled streets to give battle under the walls, the hill an advantage. Enemy cavalry couldn't charge--the ground too enclosed.

Luciano Manara on the left wing took a position at the beautiful Valmontone gate and sent down 150 of the Brigade across ravines, up through vineyards and hedges against Colonel Novi's men. The Neapolitans fled at once.

The main attack came on Garibaldi's right wing. The Legionaries, joined by Luciano Manara, drove back the Neapolitan infantry, repulsed a cavalry charge in the road and attacked hostile houses not far below the Roman gate, bursting in through doors and windows.

The Neapolitans fled, throwing down muskets.

Fiery Nino Bixio and Swiss revolutionary Gustav Hoffstetter attracted attention as great fighters. They brought to Garibaldi a score of trembling prisoners, hands clasped, knapsacks crammed with religious articles. Garibaldi let them all go, impressed by their incapacity. He would remember 11 years later.

The Lombard Brigade found the monastery door locked, the monks had taken the keys. Manara and Dandolo blew the door. The Brigade sacked rooms, lit tapers and paraded around in monk's robes, sparing the chapel and library.

Recalled in haste once again, they marched through the night of May 10-11--one month since she'd seen Peppino. The wounded were carried in carts. They arrived in Rome in the morning, thirsty, exhausted.

The Red Shirt had gained popularity. Garibaldi ordered a Red Shirt for every private of the regiment--that's 2000 Red Shirts. Women at spinning wheels spun red wool into shirts.

French diplomat Ferdinand de Lesseps who would construct the Panama Canal came to Rome and negotiated with Mazzini an armistice of 15 days she wouldn't have agreed to--French forces stationing themselves outside Rome to defend against Neapolitans and Austrians. Mazzini agreed. Not a word was exchanged about the pope's restoration.

De Lesseps: "More and more the defense of Rome seems to be in foreign hands."

Mazzini: "Papal propaganda."

"Which is powerful in France. Louis Napoleon must have the Catholic vote. We suggest a Roman commander-in-chief of your army. General Rosselli is Roman."

Mazzini agreed.

"What about Garibaldi?"

"He's General of Division of part of the army and will serve under Rosselli."

Negotiating in good faith, de Lesseps was a decoy--the day he'd been charged in Paris, Louis Napoleon wrote to General Oudinot:

"Our military honor is at stake. I will not suffer it to be compromised. You may rely on it being reinforced."

Then Louis Napoleon sent the great engineer General Vaillant to Rome with orders to disregard de Lesseps, power to supersede Oudinot if necessary.

Mazzini capitalized on the armistice by sending 10,000 troops to drive the Neapolitans out of Roman territory--exactly what Garibaldi had wanted to do several days before.

Rosselli marched too slowly, so Garibaldi dashed about in front, locating and dislodging King Ferdinand and his troops, and waited for Rosselli to lumber up. King Ferdinand retreated across the frontier. Rosselli sent Garibaldi with 2,000 troops to keep contact, not attack. The officer in command was Marochetti, who'd fought in Montevideo. Garibaldi attacked. Barely holding against superior numbers of infantry and cavalry in the vineyards and undulating ground on both sides of the Valmontone road, Garibaldi sent Ugo Bassi back to Rosselli for reinforcements. Rosselli's reply: "The men haven't had their soup."

Angelo Masina wasn't with his young cavaliers on the Valmontone road when they met the head of a long cavalry column and flew back at a gallop. Garibaldi and Aguyar rode out and turned their horses sidewise across the road, sat immovable.

"Halt! Halt!" Garibaldi and Aguyar were ridden down and buried in a melee of horses, men. Garibaldi couldn't get up. The Neapolitans came crashing in with sabers.

A body of the Legion's infantry composed of 12- and 14-year-old boys opened fire from the roadside orchards. Some boys rushed forward, dragged Garibaldi and Aguyar clear. Horses on the road completely blocked it, preventing advance or retreat. The Neapolitans fell back under fire from the boys in the orchard.

Rosselli arrived with the bulk of the army.

King Ferdinand retreated across the Pontine marshes to Terracine and Naples by way of the coast, leaving behind his wounded.

Garibaldi's plan now was pursue the Neapolitans and invade Naples. At a meeting with Mazzini and Rosselli, Garibaldi made the prophetic remark that victory under the walls of Capua would win independence of the whole peninsula. Rome, Garibaldi said, was impossible to hold for long. They didn't have enough men to hold so long a line of walls, fortifications. If Oudinot couldn't take Rome with 40,000, Louis Napoleon would send 100,000. The city must be evacuated, the government withdraw to the mountains with a small part of the army, while he lead the greater part into the Kingdom of Naples. Mazzini didn't consider Garibaldi's plan.

Garibaldi and soldiers in the southern front reached Rome on June 1st. Suffering from an attack of rheumatism and a fever, Garibaldi took to bed in his room on Via delle Carozze 59.

35. HOUSE OF THE FOUR WINDS

A French Battery firing on the Janiculum defences

She heard Peppino had been killed.

The Neapolitan soldiers who'd seen Garibaldi go down and trampled on the Valmontone Road believed he was killed and spread the news among papal supporters, Catholics in France. The Garibaldi appearing in battle several days later was an impostor, some man resembling Garibaldi substituted to maintain morale. Anita Garibaldi agreed to take this impersonator as her husband to help the cause, "as is to be expected from a devoted and immoral revolutionary woman."

She was four months' pregnant, the fever she'd caught in Rieti intermittent. She put on the silk dress and fancy hat she'd made, practiced Castillian Spanish and haughty manners of a rich lady of Spain. Captain Origoni, primary organizer of the Italian Legion in Montevideo, agreed to escort her--by ship to Livorno, then coach to Rome. Donna Rosa pleaded with her, the children cried. She left the children the last time to her husband's mother.

General Oudinot had written to Mazzini: "I defer the attack of the place until Monday morning [June 4]."

On several occasions since April 30, Garibaldi pointed out the necessity of fortifying the villas. On June 2nd, General Rosselli told the 400 men holding the villas they needn't be on the alert until Monday, June 4.

Midnight June 3-4, after crossing the Tiber to the north, a column of French troops drove the defenders into the Porta del Popolo. General Vaillant with another column blew a breach in the boundary wall, poured over the ruin, seized the Villas Corsini and Pamfili and the Vascello at the city gate, and surrounding gardens and groves of evergreen oak.

Three o'clock in the morning of his arrival from the southern front, bout of arthritis and fever, Garibaldi was awakened by a roar of cannon, rushed out and leapt on his horse which Andrea Aguyar had saddled and waiting.

"Wake up Masina and the Lancers."

Bells clashed from campaniles, drummers beat the broken beat of the alarm. Angelo Masina, 33 years old; Daverio, Garibaldi's chief of staff, 34; Luciano Manara, 24; Mameli, composer of Italy's war hymn, 18--buckled on their swords. Garibaldi, 42 years old, assembled his troops in the great piazza of St. Peter's. They started for the Janiculum.

Steep, shady lane lead to the San Pancrazio gate, mount the hill by a precipitous path and steps overshadowed on both sides by old palaces, gardens--main arteries that during the month of June would feed the battle on the Janiculum, dawn to dusk filled with soldiers, civilians rushing up and wounded dragging themselves down. Garibaldi and the Legion arrived at the San Pancrazio gate at 5:30 a.m.

The ground in front of the Villa Corsini sloped down. From the front of the stairs to the garden gate ran a drive bordered on each side by stiff box hedges six feet high. At the bottom of this boxed avenue, walls of the Pamfili-Corsini enclosure ended in an acute angle--at this apex, this death angle, stood the garden gate. Rushing through the gate five abreast, the defenders then had 250 yards to run up the narrow, boxed garden path to the villa. Immediately in front of the villa was a wall covered with orange pots; the French sheltered, fired from behind. The Villa Corsini had a wide outer staircase, men and horses could climb to the second-floor balcony, the villa's entrance.

In the glorious bright sun of morning and sweltering cloudless noon, onlookers grouped around the inside of the gate-house. A band played the Marseillaise, Dutch artist Koelman peered between sandbags.

Mounted on his white horse just outside the gate, within the line of fire, bullets piercing his poncho, Garibaldi waved in group after group of workers, students and aristocrats.

"Avanti!"

Passing five abreast through the gate, they were mowed down and driven back. Angelo Masina was carried out bleeding from his left arm.

"Take him to the hospital."

The Legion stormed up the double staircase on their horses, gained the balcony, crashed through the windows and bayoneted the French in the drawing room. Riderless horses flew down the steps. The dead piled up in open loggias on the villa's west side.

At 7:30 a.m., Garibaldi issued a bulletin: "The Corsini is in our hands."

French reinforcements counterattacked, taking the Corsini. The defenders lost 1,000 out of 6,000. Daverio, physically and morally the image of Francesco Anzani, was killed. Angelo Masina, arm bandaged, returned to fight. Nino Bixio galloped up the villa's outer staircase, charged through drawing rooms and came out on the farther balcony overlooking the Pamfili grounds under a shower of bullets, one hitting him in the side.

"I think I'll be all right."

The sun was setting when Luciano Manara and his Brigade arrived at the gate. Roselli had held them up.

"Avanti! Avanti!"

Luciano Manara, Gustav Hoffstetter, Enrico Dandolo lead 400 five abreast through the narrow gateway. Under a shower of bullets, they spread out right and left of the box hedges then rushed up the slope, plumes streaming behind. Thirty paces from the villa, they stopped, knelt and opened fire. Manara watched the slaughter ten minutes before sounding the retreat.

Garibaldi ordered the gunners on the walls to concentrate fire against the Corsini facade. The defenders held the Vascello, Casa

Giacometti.

His arm bandaged, Angelo Masina with 40 Lancers rushed in. The spectacle of Angelo Masina charging up the villa steps broke the discipline of onlookers on the walls. Citizens, gunners, artists, infantry of the spent regiments--all flooded through the gate, ran over bodies, arms and charred debris. They joined the preparations for defense.

French batteries raked them. Regiment after regiment of Oudinot's 20,000 advanced through the pine trees, tossing long shadows in the evening light. The French retook the Corsini. Boy-poet Mamelli was killed. Garibaldi wrote to Mamelli's mother:

"He was carried out past me, gravely wounded but radiant, his face shining because he'd shed his blood for his country."

The defenders fell back on the Vascello.

Angelo Masina stayed behind. He was hit riding up the Corsini's steps. Horse rearing, body arching, he fell slowly, dead, across the marble steps. During the rest of June, Italian bullets from the Vascello and French cannonballs from the Corsini sang day and night over Angelo Masina's whitening bones.

Darkness closed in. Garibaldi's white poncho moved like a moth on the road amid the last flashes of the dying battle.

Garibaldi transferred his headquarters to the Villa Savorelli, just inside the Pancrazio gate. The villa towered over the gate, though in the line of fire commanded a view of the country all around. Officers occupied the grand salon; Garibaldi and Luciano Manara, chief of staff now, small side rooms. At daybreak the officers helped themselves to good black coffee and plenty of cigars, then gathered around Garibaldi on the pavilion, small wooden balcony off the upper floor. Always the first on the pavilion, Peppino was greeted immediately by French sharpshooters, and threw them a glance while lighting his cigar. June 21, the Villa Savorelli crumbling to pieces, Peppino wrote to her:

"I know you have been and perhaps still are ill. I must see your writing and that of my Mother to lift my anxiety. The Gallo-monks of Cardinal Oudinot are satisfied with firing cannonades against us and we are so accustomed to it that we pay it no attention. Here the women and children run after the cannonballs, struggling to own them. We are fighting on the Janiculum and the people are worthy of the greatness of their past. One hour of one's life in Rome is worth a century of life."

36. END OF A DREAM

She was on her way to hours, days in Rome worth a century of life.

The first leg, from Nice to Livorno, was simple--pay the boat fare, keep an eye on her box. In Tuscany she attracted attention of agents, spies. In her best Castillian Spanish instilled with desperation, breathing heavily, animating her otherwise straight face, raising her brows, smiling falsely as a way of appearing nervous, she told the Austrian soldiers that her brother--Origoni nodded somewhat stupidly--and she were on their way to Rome to visit her husband wounded on the banks of the lower Tiber while fighting with 6,000 Spanish crusaders for the pope's--bowing her head--restoration. The Austrians let her through. French officials stopped her coach, looked her up and down--she was too elegant for an anti-papist.

The French army, supported by a train of siege guns and a corps of engineers directed by General Vaillant, increased to 25,000, then 30,000. Vaillant's trenches approached closer, closer, filled with sharpshooters who blew the walls and then easily climbed over the rubble. The French mounted batteries and shelled Garibaldi's position and the city, especially slums of Trastevere. When a bomb exploded there, citizens shouted: "*Ecco un Pio Nono!*" Pius IX had become an exploding bomb.

Mazzini spread the pathetic idea that the newly elected French

Assembly would reverse Louis Napoleon's foreign policy.

Roman regiments decimated in the attacks on the Villa Corsini, reduced to 7,000, engaged in fierce hand-to-hand fighting, losing officers one by one, for a while holding the Vascello and the bastions of the Janiculum. Garibaldi erected a battery against the enemy's flank on the rubbish heap of Monte Testaccio, dumping ground for broken crockery in the days of the Caesars.

Day and night the storm of lead and iron swept over Angelo Masina's body stretched across the Villa Corsini's marble steps.

Garibaldi stayed off the pavilion now, constantly making the rounds where the fire was hottest, restoring enthusiasm with a word, "*Coraggio...*" While a shell burst nearby, he stood tall as a statue over his prostate companions. Count Ulise Balzani, young line regiment officer, wrote to his brother, Count Ugo--he was sleeping on the ramparts where the men lay bivouacked and at dawn opened his eyes, half-aware that a horse was stepping tenderly across his body, when "I had a vision of the rider's face looking down at me out of masses of curling golden hair. It imprinted on my brain one of the noblest things in art or nature I've ever seen."

Coach passengers to Rome walked the last stretch, entered through the eastern gate. Up ahead, all around, she saw the destruction and heard French cannon booming over the hills. Captain Origoni rushed her along, guiding her close to buildings. She saw more Red Shirts than ever, the remaining 1,000 wore Red Shirts. She stopped in front of St. Peter's-in-Montorio, which was a shambles.

"Come along, do come along. No use getting killed here."

"My dear, what do you think of the way the French, as good Catholics, arrange their churches?"

She found Count Ulise Balzani's vision. Not a word how or where. She probably had Peppino's address in Trastevere. He wasn't there. His last headquarters, Villa Savorelli, was rubble.

Red Shirts were camped behind the Aurelean Wall, cannon mounted on neighboring Pino Hill. A modest house, Villa Spada, stood by itself in a small garden being bombarded front and flank. Garibaldi and a few staff officers were eating hard bread, drinking wine and water, on the third floor.

She appeared at the door, Origoni close behind.

Peppino rushed to her, picked her up. "Gentlemen, this is my Anita. We have another soldier to fight for Rome."

Later on in his room in Trastevere, one candle burning, her fingers found his side wound. "I cannot live without you."

Dr. Ripari arrived on his nightly round, prescribed for her recurring fever.

With her companion of the same color and culture, Andrea Aguyar, she rode to the Protestant cemetery at the foot of Monte Testaccio, burial place of the heretics--no names to mark their bones. She and Aguyar walked under the cypresses.

The Legion's horses were stabled in the great courtyard of Prince Torlonia's palazzo. She and Aguyar gave the children rides. She followed the wounded being carried through the streets to the hospital, formerly the pope's palace. She gave the wounded flowers, books and walked with them through the gardens, and asked the gardener to set off the water-works. The gardener opened all fountains, then handed her flowers.

Princess Belgiojoso tended to the wounded. Margaret Fuller sat in the pavilion where the pope used to give audience, reading to the wounded of Luciano Manara's Lombard Brigade. The sun went down over Monte Mario. White tents of the French light horse gleamed among the trees.

Two days after her arrival (June 29-30), Romans celebrated the feasts of Sts. Peter and Paul with bonfires, rockets going up, candles burning in every window and St. Peter's dome ablaze with colors. A violent rainstorm--thunder, lightning--extinguished the bonfires, only light from St. Peter's remained. She watched from the window in Peppino's room.

Did she see action in Rome? Not a word has been written about that. Plenty of opportunity remained. French light cavalry blocked food convoys from coming in. Dashing Roman artist Nino Costa and some of the Legion's best horsemen rode out to get food into the desolate, solitary Campagna--its vast spaces and sweeping lines of distant purple hills called to mind the *pampas* of Rio Grande. They drove 300 head into Rome.

General Oudinot chose the night of the feast for his last assault.

Did she see the detachment of Luciano Manara's brigade march off into the blinding rain, riflemen struck down by bombs, the rest knee-deep in mud plod to the *Casa Merluzzo* bastion to defend the house and open breach below? Their leader was boy-officer Emilio Morosini, 18 years old, his angelic goodness the model and wonder of the whole brigade, and Garibaldi.

Two hours past midnight, the rain stopped. Night was dark as the grave. French soldiers rushed up the breach and stormed the *Casa Merluzzo*, wounding Morosini. Four of his men carried him off into the darkness on a bloody litter.

A second column of French soldiers passed along the inside of the walls to the Aurelean Wall, storming by bayonet, then rushed the *Villa Spada*. The few riflemen carrying Morosini fell in with this column, waved the white flag of surrender. The French continued to shoot--Oudinot had ordered all killed. Morosini stood erect, was hit, fell and died.

This French column attacked the *Villa Spada's* garden gate. Luciano Manara and his sharpshooters turned out to defend. The French columns' first onslaught put many defenders to flight--they rushed about in panic, in the darkness.

Garibaldi, his men behind him, sprung out and threw themselves headlong on the attacking French, checking their advance. The runaways turned back. Emilio Dandolo described Garibaldi:

"I saw Garibaldi spring forward with his sword drawn, shouting a popular hymn. In the thick of the melee, he sang and struck about with his heavy cavalry saber, which the next day was seen covered with blood. Behind him the Red Shirts pressed into battle, fought hand-to-hand with primeval rage. In the last hour before dawn, the whole space between the Pino and city gate was a swaying mass of men killing each other with butt and bayonet, lance and knife. The next day the French generals saw the ground covered with red pennons of lances still grasped in the hands of the slain."

In the golden dawn, fresh light of morning stood the Alban, Soracte and Lucretilis Hills, the defenders' cannon silent and overturned, wheels lying among corpses.

The battle raged again. French soldiers surrounded the *Villa Spada*.

Luciano Manara and the remnant of the Brigade shut themselves in, defended from the windows. Cannonballs smashed the villa. Bullets of the Vincennes chasseurs hissed through the shattered windows.

The air inside was filled with smoke, gunpowder. Feet slipped on the bloody pavement. Luciano Manara passed from one room to another. "Keep it up. *Coraggio*..." He was standing at a window looking out at the French planting a cannon--a shot from a carbine passed through his body.

"I'm a dead man." To Emilio Dandolo: "I commend my children to you."

His supply of munitions running low, Garibaldi lead a last desperate charge. As on the night before it was cold steel, again

Garibaldi fighting in front and dealing death with his heavy sword.

Gradually the fire slackened. At midday a truce was called for the gathering of the dead, wounded.

One of the last bombs hit and killed faithful Andrea Aguyar crossing a street in Trastevere.

On his deathbed, Emilio Dandolo beside him, Luciano Manara said to Dr. Ripari: "Oh, Ripari, let me die quickly." To his friend Dandolo: "Bring up my sons in the love of religion and their country. Carry my remains into Lombardy with those of your brother." Dandolo cried. "Does it grieve you so much that I die? It grieves me also."

Garibaldi was summoned to the Capitol. The Assembly was discussing the question of surrender. It rose, cheered Garibaldi. "To the Tribune!"

"All further defense is impossible. Errors have been made but this is not a time for recriminations. Let us leave Rome with all the armed volunteers who are willing to accompany us. Wherever we shall be, there will be Rome."

The Assembly resolved to cease from a defense but remain at its post. Mazzini resigned. Garibaldi was vested with supreme plenary powers as commander-in-chief of the Roman army. Date of official surrender was set for July 3rd. She and Peppino decided to leave on the 2nd.

On the eve of departure, they dined with Gustav Hoffstetter. The Swiss revolutionary described her:

"She was a woman of about 28 with a very dark complexion, interesting features and a slight, delicate figure. But at first glance one recognized the Amazon. At the evening meal to which the general invited me, I could see with what tenderness and attention he treated his wife."

Next afternoon volunteers gathered in the piazza of St. Peter's.

She wore the legionaire's uniform--Red Shirt; baggy pants tucked into her boots; large, round hat with black feathers. Captain Vecchi escorted her. She rode to a house with a sign lettered, "Seamstress." She asked Vecchi to wait. She came out with all her hair cut. "The seamstress had the scissors and did it for me. I left her the braids in payment."

Twelve thousand crowded into the piazza of St. Peter's, the whole space paved with human faces, even to the Vatican door. The troops stood in the middle, hardly able to keep footing. Mothers pulled their sons away, boys hid in the ranks. A cheer went up from Via del Borgo. All eyes turned toward the mouth of the narrow street. Hands, handkerchiefs waved.

Her black feathers rose from the swaying crowd. Citizens rushed her and Peppino from all sides. Slowly, with difficulty, they reached the Egyptian obelisk in the middle of the piazza and turned their horses. Their staff joined them. Garibaldi signaled with his hands. He signaled a second time, then a dead silence came over the square:

"Fortune, which betrays us today, will smile on us tomorrow. I am going out from Rome. Let those who wish to continue the war against the stranger come with me. I offer neither pay nor quarters nor provisions. I offer hunger, thirst, forced marches, battles and death. Let him who loves his country in his heart and not with his lips alone follow me."

Rendezvous for departure was the Lateran Palace, residence of the popes, that evening.

Around six o'clock, she rode across St. Angelo bridge, passed the ruins of the Forum and Coliseum, and entered the open space around the Lateran Palace. In her sight now was the Triclinium of Leo III, mosaic popes and emperors kneeling together in receipt from divine powers the insignia of their right to rule the world; basilica of San Giovanni in Laterano, row of colossal statues towering over the facade, gigantic bishops and doctors leaning forward cursing the heretics. In the enchanted gardens of their enemies awaited Ciceruacchio, crafty, jolly, beside his 13-year-old son; Ugo Bassi in Red Shirt and crucifix, hair over his shoulders, manuscript of a religious poem in a leather bag around his waist, mounted on the spirited English horse Garibaldi had given to him. Four thousand other volunteers waited in the palace's vast open space, ready to march.

Citizens stood on carriages, on each other's shoulders. At eight o'clock, Garibaldi gave the signal to march.

The column of men, wagons and one cannon marched out in order under the ancient gateway, then through Porta San Giovanni. Captain Culiolo, nicknamed "Leggero," limped at the end of the column, and stopped at the gate.

PART IV: THE RETREAT

(July-August 1849)

37. THE HUNTED

She rode in silence through the Campagna.

Officers whispered orders. All light, including cigars, was forbidden. Tomb of an ancient Roman, line of ruined aqueduct hove dimly in sight, then disappeared. They marched south, as if heading for the Alban Hills, then Garibaldi ordered a sudden turn east toward the Sabine Hills and Tivoli. The Sabine's great forest of olives glittered in the rising sun. They reached Tivoli at seven in the morning. They'd given the French the slip.

How beautiful Tivoli, rising above groves and waters, Anio waterfall leaping from mountain to plain, trees and gardens hanging on the precipice beneath the Temple of Sibyl kept green by the spray, resonating with the ancient fall's thunder. Above her perched the old town, its towers set to watch Rome.

She rested among the olive trees. The men slept in the shade, some gazed back over the fading Campagna, St. Peter's dome still visible.

She received the women of Tivoli. They wanted her to ride with them to the Villa d'Este. The fountains played water games in the enchanting gardens. Then they all rode to Hadrian's villa, walked among the ruins.

Peppino rode out alone, covered every inch of ground of the night's march. His objectives were to rouse the people of Central Italy and to reach Daniele Manin in Venice. Circumstances would decide which objective they followed. Whatever direction they followed, they'd be met and pursued by four armies totaling 86,000 men. In Tuscany and the papal states alone--30,000 French; 12,000 Neapolitans; 6,000 Spaniards; 15,000 Austrians; 2,000 Tuscans. To the north lay the bulk of the Austrian army, to the east Austrians and Neapolitans, to the south the main body of Neapolitans and Spaniards already moving to cut them off if they turned toward Naples, to the west the French in Rome who'd begun sending expeditions against them, though in the wrong direction. Against these armies which had nothing to do but hunt them down, they had 80 rounds of ammunition per man.

Garibaldi decided to march north into Umbria, Tuscany and the Romagna. Austrian armies occupied these districts but the people were more likely to rise than those in Naples or the Abruzzi.

Wagons were changed for cattle and oxen, making food "walk"--they left the roads, ranged the bare Apennines. Marches were of irregular length, by day, by night. Camp was broken at odd hours, often at sunset. A feint carried out in the presence of the enemy or public was quickly followed by a feint in another direction. Garibaldi let out information exaggerating their numbers. Cavalry scouts kept him informed of the enemy miles away. Screen of horsemen always on the move 10, 20, 30 miles away from the column bewildered the opposing generals.

After taking control of Rome on July 3, the French immediately cut down all tricolor flags, prohibited all assembly and cuffed youths and other civilians who insulted the French in the streets. Dr. Ripari was arrested, other prominent Republicans executed.

Just before sunset of July 3rd, she and Peppino rode vanguard out of Tivoli toward the Neapolitan frontier.

From information supplied by clerical spies, the French, Spanish and Neapolitan generals believed Garibaldi was heading for the Abruzzi.

After marching one and a half hours, she and Peppino wheeled the column sharply to the left, doubling back on their tracks, turned northeast and crossed a mule track over a high spar of the Lucretilis Mountains. She struggled over broken ground through Italy's vineyards and olive groves, Peppino hoisting their baggage to the mountaintop, then down again into the Campagna. She saw the sunrise over Monte Retondo, 12 miles from Rome, nearer to it than Tivoli. The rearguard halted at Mentana.

Sentries posted at the town gates and on top of the hill west of town stopped clerical spies trying to leave. Inhabitants were served with requisition notices--food and wine for 4,700, to be paid for by paper money printed under the Roman Republic. The inhabitants wouldn't accept such money. Monks in the monastery refused to contribute. She and Gustav Hoffstetter rode up to the monastery. Hoffstetter wrote in his diary: "The monks were terrified of Anita and produced food and wine." On the road to Orvieto the column passed a peasant woman's house, a soldier stole a chicken. Garibaldi rode up as the woman was protesting. He ordered the thief shot. Some soldiers rode up.

"I've executed a looter, as I warned I would."

It was July 4th, Peppino's 42nd birthday. She and Hoffstetter arranged a birthday fete, roasting eight oxen on spits made from branches. Around the campfire, while she sewed a new tent, Peppino told the story of her miraculous escape in Rio Grande.

"From the moment Anita ascertained that her husband wasn't among the dead, her one thought was of flight. Taking advantage of the victory celebration of her drunken guardians, she reached a farmhouse undetected and two unknown sisters gave her shelter. At nightfall Anita dared leave and disappeared into the forest. Only one who has seen the immense forests which cover the *Serra do Espinasso* and who is acquainted with their colossal *tacuari*, those true pillars of this magnificent temple of nature, can conceive of the difficulties which this courageous Brazilian woman had to overcome on her flight from Coritibani to Lajes over a distance of 60 miles. The few inhabitants of this region were hostile to the Republicans and had taken up arms since the last Republican defeat in order to ambush the fugitives in the most dangerous passes. Was it due to her lucky star or rather to the courage with which she bravely faced all difficulties I don't know, but those waylayers fled before her! Indeed they fled with the anguished cry that they were 'being pursued by a supernatural being'. And so it was a superhuman sight to behold this courageous woman mounted on a fiery horse, galloping in a tempestuous night amidst flashes of lightening and precipitous, rocky ground! Four of these cowardly waylayers posted on guard at the ford of the River Canoas fled in terror and Anita made use of their flight to reach the bank of the river. But its waters were swollen by the rains and the mountain torrents could not be crossed in a canoe, as was usually done; still this fearless woman threw herself bravely into the seething waters and, holding fast to her horse's tail and encouraging it to swim across, she reached the opposite shore in safety. A cup of coffee in Lajes was the only nourishment taken by Anita in four days, until she joined the corps of Aranha in Vaccaria."

General Oudinot, Marshal Andréia of Italy, learned from clerical spies who'd been in *Monte Retondo* that Garibaldi was heading for the west coast north of Civitavecchia, planning to escape by sea.

The column followed the main road along the flat Tiber bank, then over desert hills, turned right and marched due north toward Tierni. The order was to march through the following night, so at noon they halted for a siesta of several hours in a cool, wooded valley, beside a great stone bridge.

Now began her physical decline. For 18 hours she marched through a draught-stricken area, every spring dry. Her body burned. Men slumped on their horses. The vanguard came to a roadside fountain whose waters were caught in long troughs from which animals drank.

Hoffstetter to Garibaldi: "Are the men running a risk drinking from polluted water?"

"There comes a time in all human events when faith is man's only resort. Today is such a time."

No one got sick.

In Tierni, British Colonel Hugh Forbes and his 650 men joined the column. She marveled at Hugh Forbes. Tall and lean, Forbes wore a white cotton suit and white top hat with chimney-pot crown. He was married to a young, beautiful Florentine woman, Peppino told her, whom Forbes had left in their villa in Florence to fight first against the Austrians in Venice, then the Bourbons in Sicily, recently harassing Austrians in the north again. (Fourteen years later, in the United States, John Brown would hire Forbes as military consultant.) Except for Forbes and his 650, no volunteers joined the expedition, desertions were constant and people of the country districts were hostile, supplying information to the French.

She said to people of the country: "Who are you afraid of? Do we speak German? Do we burn and rob? Are we fighting for or against you?"

Peppino said to her: "When I compare your people, those brave sons of Brazil, with my cowardly and effeminate countrymen, I'm ashamed to belong to these degenerate descendants of a very great people who are incapable of keeping the field for a month without their three meals a day."

From the village of Todi, Garibaldi sent out reconnoitering parties. A cavalry detachment captured a convoy of provisions meant for the French army, returning to camp with 5,000 poultry and 50,000 eggs--pleasant change from their usual diet of bread, salami, cheese and red wine.

She received the women of Todi in her tent set amid laurel, cypress, fruit trees.

The Austrian army blocked the road to the north, Spaniards advanced from the southeast, French from the southwest--the column was in danger of being caught between three converging armies. Garibaldi decided to turn back to Orvieto. They would be moving into the path of advancing French but from Orvieto they could march into Tuscany--the French wouldn't pursue into the Austrian zone.

Orvieto's citizens cheered the men, raising their spirits, and rushed down the slopes, bringing food and wine for which the region was famous. The French army was expected the next day, a town official telling Garibaldi: "General Morris sent word to us to prepare rations."

"Then we are just in time!"

Lookouts sounded the alarm--French regiment marching into the plain. Camp broke with great speed. Two detachments rode out. She saw her first action in Italy, commanding with Gustav Hoffstetter one of these detachments. Peppino spurred on the rearguard. She shivered, first time in her short, glorious life lost the reins, and raced about madly searching for Peppino, thinking he'd been killed. Her detachment captured wagons, then galloped up to the main force.

38. DECLINE

She marched through the pitch black night under rain falling in torrents. The mules foundered in ditches, the men lost their way in the muddy tracks. Inhabitants, awakened at midnight, were hostile. But then as it was when they'd emerged from nine days in Rio Grande's Forest of the *Antas*, immediately they were greeted by a warm morning sun. They'd crossed into Tuscany. Its wine was good. The landscape bounded on the west by the ridge of Monte Citona and on the east by distant hills around Lago Trasimene was rich in fruit, oil.

To reach Daniele Manin in Venice they had to pass a network of Austrian armies in Florence, Siena, Perugia and Ancona. Alarmed that Garibaldi's arrival would spark resistance to the occupying armies, Austrian generals placed their forces on alert in Tuscany and papal states, and their fleet in the Adriatic anchored off Ancona. The generals thought Garibaldi was trying to reach Tuscany's west coast.

She marched east with the column across Italy's central plain toward the northeast wall on which Cortona hangs, passing Cetona, Sarteano and Torrita with its pretty red brick towers, tramping to the chorus of frogs in the half-dried ditches. Of the scouting party sent to Chiusi, five miles to the right of the line of march, one was killed and two taken prisoners.

Garibaldi demanded the scouts release. The men were held.

She went into the monastery just outside Chiusi with Peppino and Hoffstetter, rounded up 14 monks and forced them, preceded by the abbot, to march into the town square at the head of the column. One priest and one citizen presented themselves: "The bishop orders you to release the monks."

"Arrest them and go tell the bishop I'll shoot the monks if my men aren't released."

She received 200 of Chiusi's prominent women. One woman around her age, 28, gave her a silk brocade dress. "It's a little too large now but can be refitted after the baby comes." She was seven months' pregnant.

Another woman of Chiusi said: "We've heard the woman passing herself as Garibaldi's wife is not only a harlot, but also a heretic." And another: "We've also heard that same woman is an angel from heaven."

"I'm telling you my husband has never harmed anyone in cold blood. Your monks will be released when our scouts are."

She showed Peppino her new dress, then packed it away in her saddlebags.

The bishop refused to release the scouts. Garibaldi took the monks as far as Filo, near Arezzo, then released them.

She felt the young girls of Montepulciano were too friendly. Even the monks were friendly, entertaining staff. "Out of fear," Hoffstetter wrote.

The monks cooked and served the food. She refused to eat. The monks had to bring her food to the dining chamber door, hand it to a staff officer--he served her.

Garibaldi spoke to the people of Tuscany:

"Rise up and fight for freedom under the people's banner which has struck fear in the Germans at Luino, Bourbons at Palestrina and Velletri, and French in the campaign in Rome. Out with the foreigner!"

"Out with the foreigner!"--words that 11 years later became Italy's national slogan.

People cheered but didn't join.

She was visibly ill.

By cutting directly across the Apennines, entering the papal states, then marching to the Adriatic, they would shorten the distance to Venice.

"There'll be rivers to ford and mountains to scale in torrid summer heat, 15,000 Austrian soldiers lay in wait and their generals are foxes--but we'll outfox them. Get some sleep, I'll be with you soon." Then Peppino rode out to reconnoiter. She couldn't sleep, he was with her soon.

They marched north to Castiglione Fiorentino, turned west. Austrian general D'Aspre believed they were aiming for the east coast.

The column swung around in a semi-circle, reached Arezzo. Its gates were closed. Its national guard prepared to stop them. Hoffstetter advised taking the town.

"We would suffer some wounded who would have to remain behind and they would be shot."

They marched east through a sun-baked, waterless gorge and

entered a valley close to the Tiber's source. She relieved her thirst.

The valley was exposed, so they retreated to a wooded slope filled with rivulets and rested before attempting to climb up Monte Luna, so steep the Austrians didn't guard it. Desertions mounted. Polish revolutionary Müller, commander of cavalry, deserted with 60 horsemen.

"Cowards!" she called them.

Of Garibaldi's staff, Hoffstetter, Ciceruacchio and his son remained. Ugo Bassi had fallen ill at Cesti but managed to slip through the French lines. Captain Culiolo--"Leggero"--caught up, limping heavily.

She slept inside the walled grounds of two small monasteries, under a bower of evergreens. Patriots of the Tiber Valley came up the hill, offered their services.

"This time things have gone badly. But the bloodshed in Rome will be productive and I hope in ten years at most Italy will be free."

They climbed the gigantic spirals of Monte Luna. Riding in front, Hoffstetter looked back--farms sprinkled over the steep mountainside; troops winding up like a long beautiful snake through scattered oak copses; she riding beside Peppino, his white poncho streaming out in the breeze; Angelo Masina's remaining lancers; baggage mules reduced to 40; majestic herd of white bulls with long curved horns. From the top of Citerna Hill they watched Austrian divisions, thousands of men, pour into the valley below from several directions, white columns crawling over the green plain, each ignorant of the other's movements. A road, ladder, climbed the mountain wall on the far side of the Tiber--they had to reach the foot.

The Austrian generals believed every road out of the Tiber Valley was blocked, their map not showing the road up the Trebaria Pass. Garibaldi's guide pointed to the road. At the foot of the Pass lay San Giustino--they would reach it by secret night march. False afternoon attack in Monterchi, leaving a screen of men on Citerna Hill captured the Austrians' attention.

In the falling dusk the main column descended the hill's northern slope, forced march in single file through the black night, one division going around by the road and bridge to San Sepolcro, the rest moving in a straight line across the Tiber's sandy fords.

She lost her tent. Some of the men lost their way, were captured and shot. Several 12- and 14-year-old boys were captured. When asked who they were, the boys replied: "Soldiers of Garibaldi, our chief and father."

The boys were shot.

After avoiding the armed forces of four nations for 26 days, they were forced to fight at St. Angelo in Vado against Archduke Ernst's army. She wasn't with the rearguard sabered in the streets. She retreated with most of the men.

Among the trees of Macerata where Captain Bueno, companion from Montevideo, deserted and went over with 20 men, and the best officers out of action, two Red Shirts packed a bed of leaves. She sank in, exhausted, running a high fever, thirsty and in pain.

Peppino sat beside her, holding her hand. A few officers nearby talked with Ugo Bassi.

"I wish I had the courage to spirit her away and save her."

"She means as much to every man in the column as she does to her husband." Ugo Bassi said: "She told me, 'I love my children, they're constantly in my mind and I miss them dreadfully but I'm here, you see, because I love Peppino more than any other creature in the world.' "

She fell asleep.

Peppino crept to the edge of the forest of beeches, watched, thought. Their chances of reaching a port, seizing ships and embarking for Venice were remote now. The moon in its first quarter, he fixed his glass on the tri-peaked bulk of Mount Titano pressing against the sky, San Marino's crenellated walls linking her angular watchtowers that sat upon the mount.

She negotiated the steep descent to the plain. She set up their tent on San Marino's frontier.

Garibaldi sent Francesco Nullo to ask San Marino's authorities to admit them. Captain-regent Belzoppi refused--the republic didn't wish to give the Austrians cause to enter. Belzoppi also blocked Nullo's return to camp.

Ugo Bassi went in. Belzoppi agreed to supply food, water. Bassi took a room in a cafe owned by Lorenzo Simoncini. From his window, eating supper, the friar saw in the light of moonlight the encircling watchfires of the Austrian army approaching from the north.

Bassi sent a messenger. But Peppino was in San Marino's council chamber with Hoffstetter. Hat in hand, free hand resting on his swordbelt, Peppino formally asked permission for his men to enter as political refugees.

"My troops shall lay down their arms in your republic."

Meanwhile, Archduke Ernst's army caught up with the troops at the frontier.

She and Hugh Forbes commanded. It was her last battle. She tried to stop the panic of men fleeing in isolated groups up the mountainside.

"Where's Peppino? Where's Peppino?"

White poncho flying behind him, flanked by Hoffstetter, Peppino raced through the gate and down the mountainside.

Forbes tried to protect her, at the same time organize the men. Gunners guarding the small cannon they'd dragged all the way from Rome fought fiercely for their gun. She wounded an Austrian officer, who cried as he fell, "Is that a woman or is it the devil?"

She and Peppino lead the remnants of their shattered band into San Marino.

Observing international law, Archduke Ernst didn't pursue into San Marino. His army camped at the frontier.

39. SAN MARINO

She sat silent under the portico of the Capuchin Monastery, wrapped in a blanket. It was July 31 (1849), 2 p.m.

Peppino sat on the steps beside her, writing his last order of the day. He strode into the monastery, stopped in front of the men:

"From this moment forward I release my companions from all obligations, and leave you to return to private life. But remember that Italy mustn't continue in shame and that it's better to die than to live as a slave of the foreigner."

He handed the order to an officer, saluted, left the cloister.

She quartered in Lorenzo Simoncini's cafe-inn. She allowed Giuditta Simoncini to send for a doctor. He diagnosed pernicious fever to which the pregnancy added a serious risk. She may have contracted malaria. In any case, she wasn't to travel under any circumstances. Giuditta Simoncini gave her a dark cotton dress worn by local peasant women. Theresa Cecchetti, Giuditta's sister-in-law, had made the dress. And the women of San Marino brought her flowers.

In a room on the cafe's top floor, Peppino read the terms negotiated between San Marino and the Austrian generals. The Republicans were to surrender arms and equipment to San Marino's authorities, who were to hand them over to the Austrians. General Garibaldi and his wife were to be granted safe passage through Austrian lines to a port where they were to take ship to the United States. The rest were to be permitted to return to their homes. Only those who committed ordinary crimes would be punished. An armistice was granted. Two San Marino officials and two of Garibaldi's officers were to be kept as hostages.

The staff refused. Their decision and hers and Peppino's was the same.

She changed out of the green brocade dress the women of Todi had given to her.

"Brocade is hardly suitable for fighting a rearguard action."

"You must be careful with the baby."

"The doctor said the fever tends to reoccur but doesn't affect the baby."

She gave Giuditta Simoncini the brocade dress.

"Please take this for yourself or give it to Theresa Cecchetti. I've worn it only once, this afternoon."

"I'll save it for you until you return."

Outside the cafe, in the light of the long wooden match Peppino used to light his cigar, he and tourist guide Zani traced a route to the Adriatic. Cesenatico, small fishing village on the Adriatic, had *bragozzi*, or fishing smacks, few Austrians and patriotic neighboring principalities.

José entreated her to stay in this city of refuge.

"You want to leave me."

She rode up to San Marino's gate at midnight, wrapped in her gray poncho, new dark cotton dress underneath worn by the peasant women of San Marino. Two hundred passed through gates kept open by the loyal porter. Where was the friar? Peppino sent an officer to fetch Ugo Bassi. He'd left the inn in such a hurry he forgot his collar, writing materials. They would be found on his bed, preserved with veneration after Ugo Bassi's glorious death in Bologna.

40. CESENATICO

She rode slowly across the dry bed of the Merecchia River just outside San Marino's northwest corner. Her horse stumbled in the blackness across a quarter mile of white stones, pools, sandbanks--marching north at first instead of east, between two columns of Austrian troops. She climbed the high mountain on the farther bank along mule tracks, up and down sides of ravines, on paths of dried waterbeds.

Gustav Hoffstetter lost his way in the Uso Valley's cleft, sold his horse, changed clothes and returned to his native Zurich.

She touched the road near the high-perched village of San Giovanni in Galilea. She was exhausted--but then suddenly she was cheered by the morning sun! Friendly townsfolk sent out bread, wine, watermelons. The rest of August 1st she raced on roads along high narrow ridges, on mule tracks across ravines. She re-entered the region of olives.

She crossed the deep valley of the Rubicon through corn and fruit trees, halting in the scattered hamlet of Murano, near its small parish church. Peppino carried her into the church. They rested. He hadn't slept in four days. All that day she called for water.

Next day Murano's authorities ordered the church re-blessed because Garibaldi and his immoral revolutionary wife had been in it.

She regained the high road. Suddenly, spreading out before her, was the plain where Caesar had crossed the Rubicon. Eight miles beyond was the Adriatic. Gazing out at the sea, Peppino's eyes lit up. They left the hills.

Once in the Romagna plain, crossing at right angles the great highway of Via Emilia, late that blistering afternoon reaching the village of Gatteo, guide Zani's work was done--he'd guided them between the Austrian lines and out of the hills. Peppino clasped Zani's hand. "Goodbye, dear Zani; I thank you for your work. In ten years I hope to see you again with better fortune."

In ten years Zani would come down into liberated Romagna, welcomed by Garibaldi.

She arrived at midnight in Cesenatico, 20 miles south of Ravenna. Thirteen *bragozzi*, fishing smacks, moored in the canal running down middle of main street. On their bows flew cherubs in swirls of drapery, blowing trumpets. Sails dyed scarlet, saffron, orange and brown furled and muffled. The fishermen were asleep, six Austrian guards dozed in the guardhouse, a few papal carabineers played cards in another barrack.

Suddenly came a clatter of horsemen, men dismounting, hammering at doors, scattering in all directions. The papal carabineers were dragged into the square. Red Shirts wanted to kill officer Sereni. Ugo Bassi pleaded for his life and Sereni was taken prisoner.

Hugh Forbes threw up a street barricade made up of carts, tables, benches at the town's inland entrance.

Peppino commandeered the 13 *bragozzi*--means to get to Venice. But he was the only sailor, so fishermen who owned the boats were hauled out of bed and coaxed to work by flat of the sword. The town was sacked for ropes, provisions. The *bragozzi* were towed down the half-mile of canal as far as the harbor entrance--two piers built of wooden piles and stones. A violent squall arose, breakers so heavy the vessels couldn't be put out. Peppino bounded onto one smack, another, another--all 13, on each lashing together two kedge anchors and fastening ropes. He would warp the *bragozzi* out, the way he'd warped the gunboat *Rivera* off the sandbank, just outside Montevideo's harbor. Peppino and a few other men jumped into the breakers, pushed a small boat, carried anchors out a proper distance. Peppino dove, sinking the anchors. Dawn broke. He swam back with ease through stormy water, gradually letting out the ropes, and leapt into the boat "like a sea god," one of the men wrote later on. The last rope--thin, made of inferior hemp--snapped. Peppino had to do the work over again, get fresh ropes and anchors.

    She sat by the shore seven hours, faint and in great pain, propped up so she could watch Peppino.

    He gave their horses to a local patriot. "Do what you will with them but never let them pass into Austrian hands."

    Peppino said to Leggero: "No matter how bravely she tries to hide her suffering I know she's suffering, and just as great is my own misery because I can do nothing to relieve her." Six in the morning, the 13 *bragozzi* set sail for Venice. An hour later Austrian troops entered Cesenatico.

41. HER DEATH

She drank Peppino's ration of water. "Water, water..."

The weather turned fine. With a favorable wind they coasted the Adriatic's Italian shore, sailing through the black night of August 2nd. The moon was two night's short of full, worrying Peppino and Leggero.

Next night her fishing smack passed Ravenna in the neighborhood of the marshes, around the lagoon district of Commachio--its beautiful red towers rose out of the middle of the inlet sea. She was 50 miles from Venice.

Ten o'clock the Austrian brig *Orestes* laying east of Goro point spotted them in the light of the moon, alerted an Austrian squadron to pursue and attack.

Peppino signaled all smacks to bear left away from the moonlight, take advantage of low tide for a dash to the beaches below the estuary.

Austrian gunboats fired. The fishermen abandoned rudders, sheets. Threats forced them back. Under heavy fire the smacks made for the beach at Magnavacca. Eight *bragozzi* were captured, 162 legionaries and Hugh Forbes taken to the prison-fort Pola on the Dalmatian coast.

Her boat carrying 30 men dashed to shore. She fell back, unconscious.

"Soon we'll be touching land..."

"Land, yes..."

Her fishing smack ran aground on a sand bar 1,200 feet from shore. Peppino carried her through shallow water to a deserted stretch of beach, gently set her on the sand. He released officer Sereni, ordered the men to scatter in twos and threes and make their way to Venice overland. He bid tender goodbyes to Ugo Bassi and Ciceruacchio and his son. All three would be captured and killed.

Peppino carried her into a nearby maize field, Leggero limping behind. She rested. Leggero spied the land.

"You'll be all right, darling..."

Leggero returned with Dr. Nino Bonnet--landowner, man of influence. Two of his brothers had served in Rome, one dying gloriously.

"Hundreds of soldiers in the area are incited to kill you by the promise of rich reward..."

Beachcomber Baramoro came up. Pointing inland across the marsh to a straw-roof hut, Bonnet said to Baramoro: "See that little cottage? Well, take my friends there while I'm off on some other business. The lady is ill, needs to be carried."

Baramoro and Peppino carried her to the straw hut. Bonnet hurried to the fishing smacks to fetch clothes, papers. Austrian long boats opened fire. Bonnet joined them in the straw-roof hut.

The area swarmed with papal troops, Austrian white coats.

Peppino, Leggero and Bonnet carried her two miles across sandy soil and low brush. She passed out, came to, passed out.

Bonnet's servant and gig waited at Cavallina farm.

She was placed in bed, took some broth with brandy. Dr. Bonnet took Peppino aside. "Crossing the Po and reaching Venice are impossible. If you wish to save your own life for your country, you must part from Anita as soon as she's safe and comfortable."

Peppino agreed, provided he go as far as the house designated by Bonnet for her accommodation--Zanetto farm, on the lake, the island's northern end.

Leggero and Peppino carried her in a cart. Bonnet hastened to Commachio--hire a boat to take Leggero and Peppino off the island.

Papal brigadier Sereni informed Austrian police that friar Ugo Bassi was staying at Luna Inn.

In his house in Comacchio, Bonnet told his sister-in-law Celeste he needed boatmen. She would hire the Tuccio brothers. Also, the police were looking for a friar at Luna Inn. Bonnet raced his carriage to the inn, found Bassi and urged him to run. Ugo Bassi was almost through the window. Austrian soldiers burst in and arrested him.

Bonnet dispatched the Tuccio brothers to Zanetto farm without revealing the identities of their passengers.

She was in agony, understanding Peppino was going to leave her.

Peppino said to Bonnet:

"You cannot imagine all that this woman has done for me, how tenderly she loves me. I owe her an immense debt of gratitude and love. Let her come with me."

Peppino changed into the business suit Bonnet brought, cut his hair.

Bonnet watched them float from shore and recede into the gathering gloom, the *Ave Maria* sounding over the lagoon's broad, still surface.

The Tuccio brothers steered a safe course north. Midnight, the brothers and Peppino carried her in the small vessel across the highway causeway, embarking on the larger southern lake. One brother recognized Garibaldi. She was abandoned three in the morning, August 4th, in a hut on one of the islands.

Celeste roused her brother-in-law, told him the news she'd heard in Comacchio. Bonnet rushed to the house of patriotic boatman Michele Guidi.

Guidi found them and carried her, Peppino and Leggero across the lagoon to Chiavacca de Mezzo, destination a dairy farm in Mandriole.

The men carried her in the boat up the bank. Michele Guidi fetched a cart and horse from the farm. Nino Bonnet stayed in Ravenna, arranging for Garibaldi's escape.

Seven-thirty in the evening, August 4th, she was carried to the Guccioli dairy farm near the scattered hamlet of Mandriole. Well-built, spacious, the farmhouse stood among vineyards, reeds and wasteland of the southern marsh coming almost to the farmhouse door.

"Take care of the children..." Her last words, thoughts were of the children.

Peppino clasped her in his arms. Good doctor Nanni arrived.

"Try and save this woman..."

"We must make a shift to get her to bed."

Farm owner Raviglia brought out a mattress. Michele Guidi, Peppino, Leggero and Dr. Nanni held corners of the mattress and carried her into the house, climbed to a room at the head of the stairs.

She died on the way up.

Laying her on the bed, Peppino saw the death look on her face. He burst into a flood of prolonged, bitter weeping. He couldn't bring himself to leave the body.

Austrian soldiers were about to overrun the farm. Rushing down the steps, Garibaldi said to Raviglia: "I beg you--give her a proper burial."

She was buried in haste in black night in a sandy waste. Dogs came to the burial ground, burrowed.

EPILOGUE

"He said to the King, 'I salute the first King of Italy.'"

Eleven years later, in 1860, she wasn't with her companions in Naples--José, of course; their son Menotti, dark-complexion, long black hair, still a deep scar on his forehead; daughter Tita's radical husband, Stefano Canzio; limping Leggero; guide Zani; Dr. Ripari; Hugh Forbes; Nino Bixio; Giacomo Medici. The famous One Thousand--exactly 1,089 volunteers including one 14-year-old boy, one woman and one veteran of the Napoleonic Wars, all of whom had known or heard about her--had put to flight 25,000 professional Bourbon troops occupying Sicily and Naples. All foreign armies except Austrians in Venice and Rome had been driven from the peninsula. Italy was officially declared a united, independent nation. After serving six months as temporary dictator of the Kingdom of the Two Sicilies, Garibaldi handed Sicily and Naples to King of Piedmont Victor Emanuel II, uniting these southern provinces with the mainland for the first time since the fall of the Roman Empire.

October 1860, near Teano, a small village 70 miles from Naples

To rendezvous with the king, Garibaldi crossed the Volturno River on a make-shift bridge of yard-wide wooden planks supported on boats, the planks hurled across the river by the Red Shirts while under fire from Bourbon troops, who then retreated toward Capua.

Garibaldi, his staff and a few regiments bivouacked in the wide valley between the Caianello and Vairano Hills. He told a few officers to go to the king, advise him of their presence, pay him homage. From out of his saddle Garibaldi unfolded his tent and set it up, then, as had been her custom, he came out and stuck her sword in the ground.

At dawn Garibaldi rode down the hill, followed by a few officers and regiment of Red Shirts, the shirts dusty and stained with blood. Garibaldi wore his gray poncho, pork-pie hat. He lifted his black silk scarf to protect his ears from the morning dew. Under his hat he'd tied her colorful handkerchief.

The prospect of clanking arms, shiny helmets, waving plumes attracted thousands of Neapolitans and farmers from the surrounding countryside. They stood on the hills, lined the roads. At the junction of two roads coming out of the hills stood the *Taverna della Catena,* shaded by poplar trees--here Garibaldi and staff dismounted and with beaming, dusty faces awaited the king.

Women rushed up to Garibaldi. He waved them away, knowing how his popularity irritated the king.

From down the road came the beating of drums. The musicians struck up the royal march. First of the royal troops arrived at the tavern: the king's corps of bodyguards armed with swords and rifles, pulling siege guns. Royalist general della Rocca advanced courteously to Garibaldi but the royal troops passed on, indifferent to him. King Victor Emmanuel II approached the tavern. He was dressed in royal purple, general's uniform covered with medals, great waxed mustache gleaming in the early morning sun. Behind the king stretched a long train of orderlies, chamberlains, courtesans and generals, including future viceroy of Naples, Luigi Farini, whose tunic was several sizes too big.

Garibaldi mounted, rode out of the shadows. He lowered his black silk scarf, took off his hat but kept her handkerchief knotted around his forehead. He said to the king: "I salute the first king of Italy."

"*Viva il re!*" shouted the Red Shirts.

The king held out his hand. "Ah, my dear Garibaldi, how are you?"

Garibaldi held the king's hand. "Well, Majesty, and you?"

"The roads were bad--" King Victor checked, reproved his horse--"but I'm looking forward to the breakfast awaiting us at Teano."

"I will leave you at the bridge, Majesty."

The two rode on together, Garibaldi at the king's left, royal troops and Red Shirts following in loose order several paces behind.

Soon each group returned to its center: in one line the Red Shirts, in the other the splendid royal uniforms shining with gold, silver and cordons of honor.

The crowd shouted, "Viva Galibardo!"

Garibaldi reigned in his horse, falling back, as a way of directing attention away from himself and to the king. Garibaldi shouted: "This is Vittorio Emmanuele II, the king, your king--king of Italy!"

"Viva, viva Galibardo!"

The king spurred his horse to a gallop. Luigi Farini galloped, too, grasping his saddle and letting go of the reins and stirrups, so his trousers pulled up until his knees were bare.

The king said to Garibaldi: "The royal army will finish off the Bourbons at Gaeta and Capua. You've been fighting a long time. Your troops must be tired. Mine are fresh."

The column reached the bridge that crossed the stream before the town of Teano. Garibaldi lifted his hat, then took the road across country while his Majesty crossed the bridge.

Garibaldi dismounted outside the village of Calvi. He went into an outhouse on the road. Menotti and Leggero posted their horses on an adjacent mound and exchanged glances of grave concern, then entered the outhouse. Garibaldi was standing beside a barrel on which his orderly had placed bread, cheese and glass of water. Garibaldi drank, spit out--"There must be a dead animal at the bottom of this well!"

All that day Garibaldi was silent. His face was filled with melancholic sweetness. Night fell--in camp Garibaldi was still silent. No one disturbed him. Standing beside his tent and her sword, he gazed up at the black night sky sprinkled with a million stars.

CHRONOLOGY of the LIFE of ANITA GARIBALDI

1821 (August) Born in trading settlement of Morinhos, province of Santa Cataria, Brazil South, subject of King Dom Pedro of Portugal. Father Bentão da Silva Ribeiro, herdsman, and mother Antonia de Jésus from São Paulo.

1828 Begins riding and gentling horses. Becomes an expert horsewoman. Cares for younger brothers while sisters attend one room school and mother does domestic work.

1831 King Dom Pedro abdicates if favor of five-year-old son. Brazil is ruled by regency. Outbreak of revolution in Rio Grande do Sul, Brazil's most southern province.

1834 (January) Father dies in horrific accident. Sister Manuela marries ship caulker in Rio de Janeiro, and sister Felicidade moves to Florianopolis to train as midwife and nurse. Anita is attacked by neighboring farmhand. Whips him across the mouth. Case brought before Justice of the Peace. Anita acquitted.

1835 Migrates with mother to seaport Laguna, southern Atlantic coast. (August) marries, arranged marriage, village shoemaker Manuel Duarte, a drunkard, who abuses her. (September) Republicans of Rio Grande, known as farrapos, break from Brazilian empire, proclaim a republic, elect Bento Gonçalves president. Is outspoken advocate of revolution.

1839 (May) Husband goes off with Imperial cavalry.

Volunteers in Laguna's hospital.

(July) Farrapos take Laguna. Meets Captain José Garibaldi, falls in love at first sight.

(July-September) Secret, wartime courtship. Is held up to ridicule, called "traitor," "the pirate's woman." (October-November) first combat, at sea with Garibaldi. Learns operation of gunboat. Sets up first-aid station. Breaks with family. People of Santa Catarina turn against Republicans. 22 Imperial men-of-war attack Laguna. Takes part in defense and evacuation of Laguna. With Garibaldi sets fire to Republican flotilla, retreats overland to south.

1839-40 Camplife. Treks through trackless forest of gigantic pines, Brazil south. First combat on land, part of expedition under Colonel Teixiera Nuñes in behalf of people of Cima da Serra, southern mountain district. (December) Battle of Santa Vitoria. Transports wounded to safety. Conceives first child in battle's aftermath, Garibaldi will claim. Marches in triumph through mountain districts of Vaccaria, Lajes, Cima da Serra. Lives briefly in house in Lajes. Its women visit, bring her gifts. (January) Battle of Corytibani. In charge of munitions. Is captured, imprisoned. Escapes, four days and nights without food through hostile territory, rejoins Garibaldi in Lajes. Her escape becomes famous, legendary. Mountain districts return to Imperial party. Republican soldiers desert. Retreats 200 miles south through forest to Malacara, joins main army. (July) Battle of San José do Norte. Cavalry commander while eight months' pregnant. (September) lives on abandoned farm in San Simon. Is attacked by marauding guerrilla, Moringue. Falls from horse. Gives birth to son, Menotti, in nearby village of Mostardos.

1841 Decides to leave Rio Grande for Montevideo. Is given herd of cattle in payment for fighting in behalf of Rio Grande. In Corral de Pedras, rounds up 900 head. Drives herd 200 miles to Montevideo with Garibaldi and Menotti. Half the herd drowns in Rio Negro river. Skins remaining head. (June) Arrives in Montevideo. Sets up and runs two-room apartment on Porton Street, near harbor. Uruguay is at war with Argentina. Montevideo besieged by sea and land next seven years. City is shelled, killing civilians. Home becomes base for freedom fighters. Supports Garibaldi's change from civilian life (salesman, school teacher) to commander of Uruguay's navy. (March) marries Garibaldi, bigamous marriage, after learning husband was killed in Rio Grande, but no proof. (June) sees husband off on perilous expedition to Corrientes, Argentina, designed to get rid of him and Uruguayan navy. Lives in dire poverty, soldier's, not officer's, rations.

1842 Organizes women of harbor district, building fortifications, caring for children, distributing food, raising money. Montevideo abolishes slavery.

1843 (May) designs and sews first Red Shirt, worn by Italian Legion, created by Garibaldi. Ostracized by upper-class women. Raises money for Legion hospital. Jealous of women of upper class. (June) gives birth to daughter, Rosita.

1845 (September) gives birth to daughter, Teresita, while

husband fights in the north.

1846 (January) Rosita dies. Joins husband in Salto with children. Meets matreros, gauchos of mountain ranges. (February) gives birth to son, Ricciotti.

1847 (December) Sails to Italy with children, Garibaldi to follow. Is precursor to revolution in Italy.

1848 Stays with friends in Genoa. Woman of leisure. (March) lives with mother-in-law in res forged requisition papers. Briefs Garibaldi in Montevideo. (June) reunites with Garibaldi. Recruits in Nice. Goes to Genoa, leaving children with mother-in-law.

(July) Returns to Nice. (September) cares for Garibaldi. Travels to Genoa again disguised, then to Livorno, leaving children with mother-in-law. Recruits 300. Accepts with Garibaldi expedition to Sicily, then to Venice. Travels to Florence.

(November) Returns to Nice. Pellegrino Rossi, Pius IX's prime minister, assassinated in Rome. Pope flees to Neapolitan Kingdom.

1849 (February) Roman Republic established. Joins Garibaldi in Rieti. Arranges with blacksmiths for weapons, lances, for each legionary. Meets friar Ugo Bassi, Legion Chaplain, and Angelo Masina. Contracts fever, returns to Nice. Pius calls to Rome armies of France, Spain, Austria and Neapolitan Kingdom to restore him to power.

(April) Rome defended. (June) Travels to Rome, disguised, and rejoins Garibaldi. Visits hospital, meets Margaret Fuller. (July) Cuts all her hair and changes into men's clothes. Leaves Rome with Garibaldi and four thousand volunteers. Retreats north, pursued by four armies, 86,000 men. Receives women of Tivoli, Todi. Pregnant, grows ill with fever, probably malaria. Fights last battle on San Marino's frontier. Retreats to Cesenatico, on Adriatic, destination Venice. (August) Attacked by Austrian gunboat. Delirious with fever, is carried to dairy farm in Mandriole, near Ravenna. Dies, seven months pregnant.

FURTHER READING

Abita, Salvatore & Fusco, Maria Antonella, *Garibaldi nell'iconografia dei suoi tempi.* Rusconi Libri, Milan, 1982.

Balleydier, A., Histoire de la révolution de Rome, Paris, 1851

Boiteux, H., *Anita Garibaldi.* Rio de Janeiro, 1933.

Bonnet, G. Lo Sbarco di Garibaldi a Magnavacca, Bologna, 1887

Campanella, Anthony P., *Pages from the Garibaldian Epic.* International Institute of Garibaldian Studies, Florida, 1984.

--Giuseppe Garibaldi e la tradizione Garibaldina: Una Bibliografiadal 1807 al 1970. Geneva, 1971

Cesaresco, Evelyn Martinengo, *The Liberation of Italy 1815-1870.* London, 1895

Collor, Lindolfo, *Garibaldi e a Guerra dos Farrapos.* Editora Globo, Brazil, 1958.

Cortés, Carlos E., *Gaúcho Politics in Brazil.* University of New Mexico Press, Albuquerque, 1974

Curàtulo, G.E., *Garibaldi e le donne.* Rome, 1913

D'Azelio, Marquis Massimo, *The Present Movement in Italy.* T.C. Newby, London, 1847

Dandolo, Emilio, The Italian Volunteers and Lombard Rifle Brigade. London, 1851

Deiss, Joseph Jay, *The Roman Years of Margaret Fuller.* Thomas Y.

Crowell Co., New York, 1969

Dumas (père), Alexandre, *Montevideo, ou une nouvelle Troie*. Paris, 1850

Dwight, Theodore. See Garibaldi

Freka, Frederick, *A Peace Congress of Intrigue, Vienna, 1815*. The Century Co., New York, 1919

Freyre, Gilberto, *Order and Progress, Brazil from Monarchy to Republic*. Edited and translated from the Portuguese by Rod W. Horton. Alfred A. Knopf, New York, 1970

Frischauer, Paul, *Garibaldi*. Kendall & Sharp, New York, 1935

Garibaldi, Annita I. [great granddaughter], *Garibaldi en América*. Buenos Aires, 1930

Garibaldi, Erika, *Qui Sosto Garibaldi*. International Institute of Garibaldian Studies, Florida

Garibaldi, Giuseppe--The Memoirs:

--The Life of General Garibaldi written by himself. With sketches of his Companions in Arms. Translated by his friend and admirer Theordore Dwight. A.S. Barnes and Burr, New York, 1859

--*Garibaldi's Memoirs from his manuscript, personal notes and authentic sources*. Elpis Melena. Edited with Introduction and Annotations by Anthony P. Campanella, Volumes I, II, Annex: *The Wars of the South American Republic*. Translated from the German *Garibaldi's Denkwürdigkeiten* by Erica Sigerist Campanella. International Institute of Garibaldian Studies, Sarasota, Florida, 1981

--*The Memoirs of Garibaldi, edited by Alexandre Dumas*. Translated and with an   Introduction by R.S. Garnett, with Contributions by George Sand and Victor Hugo. D. Appleton and Company, New York, 1931

--*Autobiography of Giuseppe Garibaldi*. Translated by A. Werner. With an Introduction by A. William Salomone. Supplement by Jesse White Mario. Volumes I, II, III. Howard Fertig, New York, 1971

--Edizione Nazionale degli scritti di Giuseppe Garibaldi, Epistolario (1834-1848) Volume   VII, (1848-1849) Volume VIII. Instituto per la Storia del Risorgimento Italiano, 1973, 1978

Guerzoni, Giuseppe, *Garibaldi*. Florence, 1882

Hales, E. E. Y., *Mazzini and the Secret Societies*. P.J. Kennedy & Sons, New York   Haug, C. James, *Leisure & Urbanism in Nineteenth-Century Nice*. The Regents Press of Kansas Lawrence, 1982

Hoffstetter, Gustov Von, *Tagebuch aus Italien 1849*. Zurich and Stuttgart, 1851

Hibbert, Christopher, *Garibaldi and His Enemies*. Little, Brown and Co., Boston, 1965   Johnston, R. M., *The Napoleonic Empire in Southern Italy, Volumes I & II*, Macmillan & Co., 1904

King, Bolton. *The LIfe of Mazzini*. E.P. Dutton & Co., New York, 1912

Mack Smith, Dennis, *Garibaldi: Great Lives Observed*. Englewood Cliffs, N.J., 1969

Mario, Alberto, *The Red Shirt*. London, 1885

Montanelli, Indro and Nozza, Marco, *Garibaldi*, Rizzoli, Milano, 1962

Parris, John, *The Lion of Caprera.* David McKay Company, Inc., New York, 1962.

Ridley, Jasper, *Garibaldi.* Viking, New York, 1981.

Sacerdote, Gustavino, *La Vita di Giuseppe Garibaldi.* Milan, 1933

Sarmiento, Domingo F., Life in the Argentine Republic in the Days of the Tyrants. New York, 1868

Sergio, Lisa, *I Am My Beloved.* Weybright and Talley, New York, 1969.

Sforza, G., Garibaldi in Toscana nel 1848. Rome, 1897

Trevelyan, G. M., *Garibaldi's Defense of the Roman Republic.* Longmans, Green and Co., London, 1912.

-- *Garibaldi and the Thousand.* Longmans, Green and Co., London, 1910.

--*Garibaldi and the Making Of Italy.* Longmans, Green and Co., London, 1912

Valente, Valentim, *Anita Garibaldi, heroína por amor.* Rio, Pongetti, 1949

Vecchi, C. A., La Italia: Storia di due anni 1848-49. Turin, 1856

Vellinho, Moysés, *Brazil South: Its Conquest & Settlement.* Alfred A. Knopf, New York, 1968.

Webster, Sir Charles: *The Congress of Vienna.* Barnes & Noble, Inc., New York, 1963.

Winnington-Ingram, H.F., *Hearts of Oak.* London, 1889

ACKNOWLEDGMENTS

Dr. Anthony Campanella laid the foundation of this book through his lifetime of work dedicated to Garibaldean studies. In the mid-1980s Dr. Campanella opened his vast archive in Sarasota, Florida and Geneva, Switzerland to me, and gave me copies of his books, including his two-volume bibliography of all published writings on Garibaldi up to 1970, with 16, 147 entries.

Also in the mid-1980s my friend and publisher Lawrence Freundlich lent financial support that facilitated travel and research in South America.

I am grateful to Ms. Irma Enriques for organizing my travel research, and for guiding and translating in libraries and archives of Argentina. I want to thank the Faillas of Buenos Aires for their hospitality. Dr. Hugo Failla, also a sailor, was a valuable source of information on the Rio de la Plata and Atlantic coastal waters, and he positioned Garibaldi as a *matrero*, gaucho of the mountain ranges.

On his travels through Italy my son Bill Valerio sent me books about Garibaldi that were particularly helpful in visualizing. Daughter Francesca Valerio provided useful images, and daughter Gianna Valerio believed and comforted.

From the beginning Maria Inês Lacey lent major support and work. She translated from numerous Portuguese and Spanish texts, traveled, researched and photographed in Laguna, Brazil and Montevideo, Uruguay. Ms. Inês Lacey helped me to understand Anita Garibaldi, from her early life in Brazil South, the importance of her father, her arranged marriage, the nature of her relationship to G. Garibaldi, to Anita's final decision to leave her children and, according to her nature, to fight, viewing Anita not as a martyr but, as Professor Philip V. Cannistraro writes, the active agent of her own destiny.

I am grateful to Professor Cannistraro for his wisdom and work in behalf of the book, and for his and his family's hospitality in New York and Pennsylvania.

Professor Ellen Nerenberg read the manuscript, like herself

made it all consistent, made sure all the Italian was correct, translated into Italian and lent hospitality, allowing me to write the final version of Anita's story in her home in Middletown, Connecticut.

Anthony Valerio's books include THE MEDITERRANEAN RUNS THROUGH BROOKLYN (new Ebook edition); VALENTINO & THE GREAT ITALIANS; CONVERSATION WITH Johnny; BART: a Life of A. Bartlett Giamatti; THE LITTLE SAILOR, a Romantic Thriller; TONI CADE BAMBARA'S ONE SICLIAN NIGHT, a memoir; JOHN DANTE'S INFERNO, a Playboy's Life; SEMMELWEIS. Mr. Valerio's short stories have appeared in the Paris Review and in anthologies and readers published by Random House, the Viking Press & William Morrow. He has taught creative writing at New York University, the City University of New York and Wesleyan University. He was a fiction judge at PEN and is a member of the Authors League.

www.ingramcontent.com/pod-product-compliance
Lightning Source LLC
Chambersburg PA
CBHW030433010526
44118CB00011B/613